D1278744

6 23
STRAND PRICE
7 00

À la carte

Book created, developed and edited in Colombia by
VILLEGAS ASOCIADOS S.A.
Avenida 82 No. 11-50, Interior 3
Bogotá, D.C., Colombia
Telephone (57-1) 6161788.
Fax (57-1) 6160020 /6160073
e-mail: informacion@VillegasEditores.com

© VILLEGAS EDITORES 2002

Art Department
ENRIQUE CORONADO

Translation
MARÍA EUGENIA MOSER

Editing
SOLVEIG WILLIAMS

Proofreader
STELLA DE FEFERBAUM

Prop Styling
ANA MARÍA GONZÁLEZ ROJAS

Kitchen assistant
PAULA RIAÑO PERESSON

Photography assistant
ALEJANDRO MONTOYA

All rights reserved
No part of this book many be reproduced, stored
in a retrieval system or transmitted, in any form
or by any means, electronic, mechanical,
photocopying, recording or otherwise,
without the prior permission of Villegas Editores.

First Edition
October, 2002

ISBN
958-8156-18-1

VillegasEditores.com

MARÍA VILLEGAS

À la carte

Director, designer and editor
BENJAMÍN VILLEGAS

Recipes and food styling
MARÍA VILLEGAS

Photography
CLAUDIA URIBE TOURI

Villegas
editores

TO THOSE WHO SUPPORTED ME

To Juan Pablo and Michelle for having been so patient and understanding during those long, tedious, and demanding hours of hard work that rightly should have belonged to them. To my parents for their unswerving support of my initiatives. To my brother and sister who, although they are far away, transmit their enthusiasm and energy for all that I undertake. To Claudia Uribe for taking the leap with me in this delightful adventure. To Ana María González for reading my mind in every detail, with such desire and extraordinary good taste. To Adriana Posada for always bringing order into any unexpected chaos. To Alejandro Montoya for the magic of his conscientiousness and his audacity to taste all the recipes. To Paula Riaño for her dedication to the project and her help with the preparations. To Rosa for her loyal assistance in the never-ending hours of hard labor. To Stella for her valuable suggestions when developing my ideas on paper. To Enrique and all the art team of Villegas Editores for their continuous enthusiasm and generosity with their time. To Laura Moser for her openhanded, professional help, and to Laura Arango for her sincerity and wholehearted support at all times.

Without the valuable and generous contribution in products, equipment, and decoration for the photographs and the production of the following establishments in Bogotá, each one by far more exquisite and select in its field, this book would not have had such a positive outcome. To all of them, I am very grateful for their confidence and patience.

Koyomad S.A. Productos Cárnicos, Productos Koller y Kopoyo Carnes y Salsamentaria, Calle 122 # 30-12 Tel. 6196260; Cachivaches, Cra. 9 # 69-26 Tel. 2498859; Eurolink, Calle 85 # 9-86 Tel. 2573676; Mónica de Rhodes, Telas, Calle 79B # 7-90 Tel. 6130510; Dupuis, Calle 79B # 7-97 Tel. 3459445; Spazio, Centro Comercial Portobello Tel. 6355301; Wabi, Calle 81 # 8-28 Tel. 2129973; Lina Pardo y Colleen Bowler, ceramistas, Calle 69 # 6-46 Tel. 2499824; Savile, Cra. 10 # 82-90 Tel. 6350675; The Tea House, Cra. 14 # 80-73 Tel. 6163289; Amago Decoración, Calle 82 # 7-42 (706) Tel. 6356474.

CONTENTS

FROM THE AUTHOR

This book was born from a dream shared with Claudia Uribe, my good friend and great photographer to make a book that would combine both our passions and have the seal of our own personal and professional identities. The dream slowly developed by means of diverse combinations: the birth of my daughter Michelle and with it the sweet anchorage to the house; the remodeling of my kitchen that invited itself to exploitation; and the numerous requests of many people to start teaching some cooking classes.

All these coincidences set up the right scenery for making this dream come true. It occurred to me that the lessons should be, not only an experimental workshop for the book, but also the acid test of my ideas and the seedbed of requests and whims. I agreed with my students that there would not be a set script, but instead, each class would be a surprise. This forced me to think, and think again, the recipes that I would submit to their judgement, trying out their feasibility and their capacity to become passionate…

Throughout the course no one dropped out!

In each two hour session we were able to explain, prepare, and taste a minimum of three recipes. The chosen formulas – simple, fast and surprising – fascinated the modern housewives and young executives of both sexes who had signed up for the classes. They were all able to impress their guests successfully and to make their partners enthusiastic.

Although all these recipes would be published, the secrets and tips that came up during the course led my students to cling on. The passionate acceptance of these details, which in the long run are part of my own culinary experience, inspired the idea of including these tips in the recipes of the fifteen sections that make up this special cookbook.

Completing the book, the production began. It had minimalist dishes, adjusted to the trends of modern times: healthful, with natural ingredients and exotic flavors; light, easy to prepare, and with a sophisticated appearance, totally fashionable. The presentation had to follow a similar tone. Nothing in the book is altered: the embellishment is simple and made by hand. The dishes were photographed as they came out from the kitchen. The visual aspect, as important as its contents and flavor, could not have been interpreted in a better way than through Claudia Uribe's authentic photographs, with which the affinity in the aesthetic conception of the work was resounding. Her pictures reflect exactly what we had both visualized in our shared dream.

MARÍA VILLEGAS

seven entrées

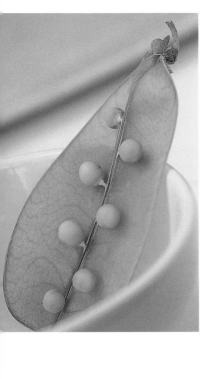

Stir-fried vegetables with coconut milk

Makes 4 servings

2 to 3 tablespoons vegetable oil
1 bunch fresh, green asparagus, cut into pieces
2 zucchini, washed, dried and cut into sticks
1 cup snow peas, cut into 1-inch slices
1 large white onion, cut in slices
2 cups white mushrooms, cut in quarters
1 red bell pepper, cut in Julienne strips
3/4 cup coconut milk
1 tablespoon sweet chilli sauce
1 tablespoon cilantro, chopped
Salt and pepper

Heat some of the vegetable oil in the wok until very hot; add the vegetables one by one, cooking them separately until fragrant. Once this is done, put them all back into the wok, and add the coconut milk, the chilli sauce, the cilantro, and salt and pepper to taste. Cover the pan briefly for about 2 to 3 minutes and serve at once.

These vegetables are also an excellent side dish.

Vegetarian spring rolls

Vegetarian spring rolls
Makes 10 to 12 rolls

3 tablespoons all-purpose flour
6 tablespoons water
1 tablespoon vegetable oil
1 medium-size carrot, cut in fine Julienne
1 small red bell pepper, cut in fine Julienne
1 package 2 ounces/60 g Vermicelli
2 cups white mushrooms or shiitake, thinly sliced
1 tablespoon fish sauce
2 tablespoons light soy sauce
1/2 teaspoon sugar
Pepper
10 to 12 wrappings for spring rolls
Vegetable oil for frying

Spring roll sauce
4 tablespoons sugar
6 tablespoons rice vinegar
1/2 teaspoon salt
1 small chilli, chopped or 1 teaspoon dry chilli flakes

Mix the flour with the water and cook over medium heat until a thick uniform paste is formed. Set aside. Meanwhile cook the vermicelli in hot water for two minutes. Strain and roughly cut with scissors.

In a separate frying pan or wok, heat the vegetable oil and add the carrot and the red pepper; then add mushrooms, and cook for 3 more minutes. Last, add the vermicelli, the fish sauce, the soy sauce, the sugar, and mix well. Season with pepper to taste. To make the rolls, put each individual wrapping with one of its ends towards you. Pour one scant tablespoon of the filling about 2 inches/5 cm from the nearest end and fold it covering the filling, and seal with a small amount of paste. Fold the sides towards the center and begin to roll firmly until reaching the other end.

Seal well with more paste. Deep-fry in hot vegetable oil until all sides brown.

Serve with the following sauce: boil the sugar with the rice vinegar and salt, until syrup is formed. Add the chilli and cook one more minute.

Serve at room temperature.

18

Blue cheese soufflé with port sauce

Makes 6 servings

1 tablespoon unsalted butter, melted
2 tablespoons unsalted butter
1/4 cup all-purpose flour
1 cup whole milk
3/4 cup blue cheese
4 egg yolks
Nutmeg, salt, and pepper to taste
5 egg whites

Port sauce
1 teaspoon sugar
Water
1/4 cup port
6 red grapes, cut in halves and seeds removed
1/3 cup red wine
1 ounce/30 g unsalted butter

Preheat oven to 400° F/200° C.

Grease a soufflé dish or 12-inch/30 cm casserole with the melted butter. In a saucepan, melt butter over low heat and stir in flour with a wooden spoon, mixing constantly to avoid mixture to brown. Remove from heat and gradually whisk in milk. Return to heat and cook, stirring constantly, until mixture thickens and boils. Remove from heat and at room temperature, add blue cheese that has been previously crushed with a fork.

Add the egg yolks one by one mixing without stopping. Season to taste with salt, pepper, and nutmeg to taste.

In a separate medium bowl, beat egg whites to soft peaks. Fold in one third to the cheese mixture and with a rubber spatula, gently fold in the remaining beaten egg whites until just blended. Pour into soufflé dish and bake for 25 minutes. Serve immediately.

Meanwhile prepare the following sauce:

Put the sugar in a small saucepan and add a little water to moisten the sugar. Place over high heat and boil until it becomes a caramel. Add port and the grapes. Cook for 3 minutes; then add the red wine and let it reduce for 4 minutes longer. Blend, and with motor running, add the butter cold and in small cubes until it has blended in completely. Serve over the hot soufflé.

This recipe works well as a side dish, without the sauce.

19

Blue cheese soufflé with port sauce

Eggplant a la parmigiana
Makes 8 servings

4 large eggplants
All-purpose flour, as needed
1$^{1/2}$ cups olive oil
2 cups natural tomato sauce
2 tablespoons fresh basil chopped
8 ounces/250 g grated Mozzarella cheese
3/4 cup Parmesan cheese to sprinkle

Natural tomato sauce
1 tablespoon olive oil
1 tablespoon white onion, finely chopped
1/4 cup white wine
10 ounces/300 g red tomatoes, peeled and chopped
1/2 teaspoon sugar
Salt and pepper

23

Cut the eggplants in thin slices, place them in layers in a colander
and sprinkle salt between each layer. Let stand for 1 hour to
remove sour taste. Wash in cold water and dry on both sides with
paper towel. Lightly coat each slice with flour.
In frying pan, heat some of the olive oil, and fry the slices of
eggplant, turning halfway, until brown. Add more oil if necessary.
Place on paper towels to remove excess fat.
In 13" by 9"/32 x 23 cm ovenproof glass or ceramic baking
dish that has been previously greased with butter, place slices to
cover bottom. Season with pepper. Top with tomato sauce and
fresh basil. Sprinkle mozzarella and Parmesan cheese. Repeat
layers in the same order until all ingredients have been used,
finishing with a layer of cheese. Bake for 30 minutes and let stand
for 30 minutes.

In a saucepan, cook oil over low heat, and sweat onion until
translucent. Add wine and let evaporate; add tomatoes and sugar
and cook for 10 to 15 minutes. Season with salt and pepper to
taste.
Makes 2 cups.

Crunchy asparagus with sesame seeds / Gyozas in dashi and mirin sauce

Crunchy asparagus with sesame seeds
Makes 12

12 fresh green asparagus
3 sheets phyllo (16" by 12"/40 x 30 cm each)
Clarified unsalted butter, see tip below
1/3 cup toasted sesame seeds

Sesame and soy sauce
2 egg yolks
1$^{1/2}$ tablespoons toasted sesame seeds
1 tablespoon soy sauce
2 tablespoons vegetable oil
1/2 teaspoon chilli oil
Salt and pepper

Cook the asparagus steamed or in boiling water until they are al dente. Strain and shock in cold water, dry with paper towel, and set aside.

Arrange phyllo sheets on waxed paper; grease the surface with clarified butter. Cut each sheet into 4 identical rectangles. Roll each one with an asparagus, leaving the tip out in the open. Sprinkle with toasted sesame seeds. Place on baking tray in preheated oven in broil and cook for a few minutes until they are brown on all sides. Remove from oven and serve hot with the following sauce:

Place egg yolks, toasted sesame seeds, and soy sauce in the blender, and blend until a smooth mixture is obtained. With the motor still running, add the oils slowly in one steady stream until they blend in completely. Season with salt and pepper to taste.

Note: To obtain clarified butter heat until the milk solids settle to the bottom. Skim the butterfat from the top and strain the clear yellow liquid into a container. This has a clear aspect; and it resists high temperatures without burning.

26

*THESE JAPANESE DUMPLINGS CAN BE BOILED, FRIED OR BROWNED, WITH
DIVERSE FILLINGS. THIS RECIPE IS CREATIVE AND WORTH TRYING*

Gyozas in dashi and mirin sauce
Makes 12 to 14

1 tablespoon vegetable oil or sesame oil
3/4 cup ground beef
6 white mushrooms, cut in very small dice
2 tablespoons teriyaki sauce
1$^{1/2}$ tablespoon cilantro, chopped
Salt and pepper
1 pinch chilli powder (optional)
12 to 14 wrappings for gyoza
1 green lettuce of your choice

Dashi and mirin sauce
1$^{1/2}$ cup water
1$^{1/2}$ tablespoon Dashi
1$^{1/2}$ tablespoon Mirin
2 tablespoons soy sauce

In a medium frying pan, heat oil over high, add ground beef and cook, stirring often, for 5 minutes, or until beef begins to brown. Add the mushrooms and the teriyaki sauce, and cook for a few more minutes. Last, add cilantro and the chilli (optional); season with salt and pepper to taste and remove from heat.

Place one wrapping for gyoza on a flat surface and add 1 teaspoon filling. (Keep remaining wrappings covered with moistened cloth to avoid drying). Brush the edges with water and fold round in half to enclose filling to form the dumpling. Seal the edges by pinching with fingertips. Repeat procedure until all the ingredients have been finished.

Cover the bottom of a steamer with lettuce leaves so that gyozas don't stick together in the bottom of the basket. Fill with water just enough to cover the lettuce. Place the gyozas on top and steam for 7 minutes. Remove with a skimmer and serve in the following hot sauce:

Boil the water with the Dashi until it dissolves. Add the rest of the ingredients.

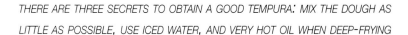

Tempura vegetables

Makes 4 to 6 servings

1 egg
1 cup cold water
1 cup all-purpose flour
1/2 teaspoon salt
Vegetables of your taste cut in thin slices or strips: mushrooms, eggplant, carrots, onion, and zucchini
Cooking oil for frying

Soy and ginger sauce
1/4 cup soy sauce
4 tablespoons water
2 tablespoons rice vinegar
1 tablespoon sugar
1 teaspoon grated ginger

28

Mix the egg with the cold water; whisk in flour and salt rapidly.
Dry the cut vegetables and dip in the tempura mixture until well coated. Then deep-fry in very hot oil for 2 to 3 minutes. Remove from skillet, and place on paper towel to remove excess fat.
Season with salt, and serve immediately with the following sauce:

Place all the ingredients in a small saucepan over medium heat, mixing until the sugar has melted completely; boil for 1 minute.
Remove from heat and serve warm or at room temperature.

five salads

Tabbouleh
Makes 8 servings

1/2 cup bulghur wheat #1
6 Roma tomatoes, chopped and without seeds
10 cups flat leaf parsley, without leaves
1 cup mint, finely chopped
3/4 cup chives finely chopped
1 small onion, finely chopped
1/2 cup olive oil
1/2 cup fresh lime juice
1/4 teaspoon Szechwan pepper
1/4 teaspoon black pepper
1/4 teaspoon ground cinnamon
Salt to taste

Wash wheat in a colander and strain well for about 15 minutes
or until dry; add the tomatoes. Mix the parsley, the mint, the
chives, and the onion with olive oil and lime juice.
In a separate bowl mix the peppers, cinnamon and salt.
Mix everything together and serve with pita bread.

32

Hearts of lettuce with blue cheese / Toasted chicken salad with sesame

Hearts of lettuce with blue cheese

Makes 4 to 6 servings

3/4 cup whipping cream
3$^{1/2}$ ounces/100 g blue cheese in small pieces
1/2 tablespoon white wine, white vinegar or lime juice
1 tablespoon cognac (optional)
Salt and pepper
2 firm Iceberg lettuce
1/2 cup chopped nuts

Whisk the whipping cream with the blue cheese until smooth and creamy. Add white wine, vinegar or lime juice, and cognac. Season with salt and pepper to taste, and pour over the lettuce previously cut in squares. Sprinkle with nuts and serve.

Toasted chicken salad with sesame
Makes 6 servings

4 skinless, boneless chicken breast fillets
1/2 cup all-purpose flour
1 egg
1 teaspoon water
1 pinch salt
1 cup toasted sesame seeds
Sunflower oil for frying
6 to 8 cups different fresh lettuce leaves cut in small pieces
2 tablespoons cilantro leaves

Honey and mustard dressing
6 tablespoons white wine vinegar
3 tablespoons honey
2 tablespoons olive oil
3 tablespoons Dijon mustard

Cut the chicken fillets in slices 1-inch thick. Dredge with flour; then in egg mixed with water and salt; last cover with sesame seeds on both sides.

Heat oil in a skillet, and fry the chicken slices for 5 minutes or until brown on both sides. Remove and let stand on paper towel and season with salt.

Meanwhile mix all the ingredients of the dressing in a small, deep bowl. Pour some of it on top of the lettuce that has been Ocut and mix gently. Place the chicken fillets hot; decorate with cilantro leaves and serve immediately with the rest of the dressing on the side.

This chicken, without the lettuce, is also a delicious appetizer.

37

Caesar salad

Caesar salad

Makes 4 to 6 serving

Croutons
1 garlic clove minced
1/4 teaspoon salt
1/4 cup extra virgin olive oil
2 cups white bread (baguette or bread loaf) cut in squares

1 egg
3 tablespoons lime juice
1 teaspoon Worcester sauce
1/4 teaspoon salt
Coarsely ground black pepper
1/2 garlic clove, small, passed through water and pressed
1 tablespoon anchovy fillet, chopped or anchovy paste
1/3 cup extra virgin olive oil
4 Romaine lettuces
1/3 cup grated Parmesan cheese

Mix the garlic clove with olive oil and let stand for 20 minutes. Put the bread cubes in a frying pan and strain over them the mixture of olive oil and garlic. Brown over high heat. Remove and let stand.

Boil the egg for 45 seconds. Remove carefully with a slotted spoon or skimmer, break, and pour it into the blender. Add lime juice, Worcester sauce, salt, pepper, garlic, and anchovy; blend until obtaining a smooth mixture. Add olive oil in a steady stream. (This can also be done with a hand mixer).

Wash the heads of lettuce and discard outside leaves. Cut the rest in 2-inch/5 cm pieces, and place them in a salad bowl. Pour half of the sauce and toss lightly. Sprinkle with the cheese, the remaining sauce, and the croutons. Serve immediately.

40

Arugula salad with pears and pepper

Makes 4 servings

8 slices rye bread
Olive oil
1/3 cup grated Parmesan cheese
2 tablespoons unsalted butter
1 tablespoon brown sugar
2 pears, peeled, cored, and cut into eighths
1/2 teaspoon ground black pepper
1 tablespoon cilantro, chopped
1 red onion, cut in thin slices
1 tablespoon balsamic vinegar
1 whole lettuce, loose leaf
$1^{1/2}$ cups arugula
1 tablespoon lime juice
1 cucumber cut in thin sticks
$3^{1/2}$ ounces/100 g blue cheese, cut in cubes

Spread the olive oil on the slices of bread and sprinkle them with Parmesan cheese. Toast in the oven until brown and crunchy.
Melt the butter in a frying pan, add the sugar, and cook for 2 minutes. Add the pears and sauté them until they begin to brown. Fold in the cilantro and the pepper; remove from heat.
In a separate skillet, heat some olive oil, add the slices of red onion, and sauté rapidly; add the balsamic vinegar and remove from heat.
Prepare the lettuce in small pieces with the arugula and mix with lime juice. Add the rest of the ingredients previously prepared, the cucumber, and the blue cheese. Toss lightly so as to not harm the leafy greens and serve with the slices of rye bread.

41

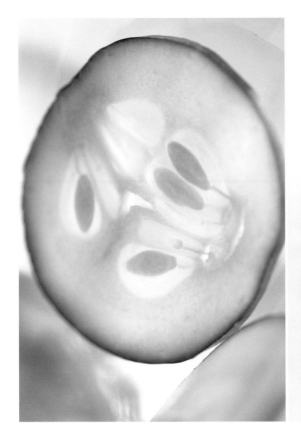

Arugula salad with pears and pepper

four soups

Portobello mushroom soup

Makes 4 servings

3 tablespoons olive oil
1 small chilli
5 Portobello mushrooms, cut in thin slices
1 tablespoon white onion, finely chopped
1/2 cup white wine
$1^{1/2}$ cups chicken broth
1/4 cup whipping cream
2 tablespoons cilantro, chopped
1/4 cup water
Salt and pepper to taste

Heat olive oil in frying or broiling pan; add the chilli and cook for
1/2 minute. Remove chilli and add portobello mushrooms; sauté
or broil over medium heat for 15 minutes to add a special flavor
which enhances the final result. Mix occasionally with a wooden
spoon. Then add salt and pepper to taste. Remove from heat and
remove excess oil (saving it for later on). Add whipping cream,
cilantro, mix well, and let stand.

In a medium saucepan, pour the oil left over from the portobello
mushrooms and simmer the onion over low heat until it becomes
translucent. Then add the white wine over medium heat, and let it
reduce for 3 minutes; add the chicken broth, and cook for 5
more minutes. Blend the mixture of portobello with the chicken
broth and the water. Season with salt and pepper to taste and
serve hot.

Red lentil soup with lime

Red lentil soup with lime

Makes 4 servings

1 cup red lentils
1 tablespoon olive oil
1 large leek
1 sprig of thyme
1 sprig of fresh oregano
2 medium-size potatoes, peeled and cut into cubes
$2^{1/2}$ cups chicken or vegetable broth
2 cups water
$1^{1/2}$ cups baby spinach, chopped
3 to 4 Tablespoons lime juice
Salt

50

Put the lentils in a bowl, cover with cold water, and let it stand for 2 hours.

Heat the oil in a saucepan, adding the white part of the leek that has been washed well, and cut into thin slices. Cook over medium heat for a few minutes until leek is tender, and begins to brown. Add thyme, oregano, potatoes, the broth, the water and the drained lentils. Cook for 40 minutes or until the lentils are tender.

Remove thyme and oregano and discard. Pour half of the soup in the blender and process to obtain a creamy purée. Pour again into saucepan with the rest of the soup and add the spinach. Cook for 2 more minutes and season to taste. Last, add the lime juice and cook 1 more minute. Serve immediately.

This soup can be prepared in advance, adding the lime juice only when served.

Mexican tortilla soup
Makes 4 to 6 servings

1 chicken breast
1 cup chicken broth
1/2 cup water
9 corn tortillas or 2 cups full of nachos or tortilla chips
Cooking oil for frying (optional)
1 tablespoon cooking oil or unsalted butter
2 garlic cloves, pressed
1/2 white onion, chopped
4 red, ripe tomatoes, peeled and chopped
5 cups chicken broth
2 corn tortillas, cut in small pieces, or a handful of nachos
Salt and pepper
2 tablespoons cilantro chopped
1 to 2 avocados, cut into cubes
3/4 cup grated mozzarella cheese
1/2 cup heavy whipping cream
2 Jalapeno peppers, sliced, without seeds and browned in oil
for 1 minute or pickle (optional)

Cook the chicken breast without the skin in the broth and the water for 20 minutes. Remove from heat and let stand. Cut chicken into bite-size pieces and set aside.

If you are using tortillas instead of nachos, cut each one into 6 triangles, fry them in hot oil and place them on paper towel to remove excess fat.

Heat the oil or butter in a medium saucepan, add the garlic cloves, onion, and a pinch of salt; sweat over low heat until they become tender and translucent. Once cooked, purée in a blender together with the tomatoes and 1/2 cup chicken broth. Return to saucepan and cook over medium heat for 15 minutes. Blend the rest of the hot broth with the tortillas; add to the tomato mixture and cook for 45 minutes more, stirring occasionally. Season with salt and pepper to taste, add chicken, and pour into a soup tureen. Sprinkle cilantro and place on top the extra nachos, the avocado, and the cheese. Serve with whipping cream and jalapeno peppers on the side for those who like them.

51

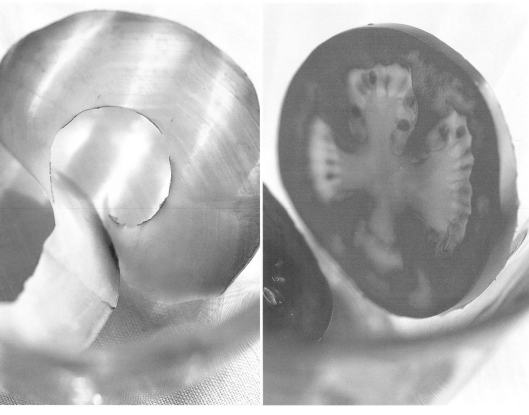

Mexican tortilla soup

Thai coconut soup

4 servings

1 package 2 ounces/60 g Vermicelli
 2 cups chicken broth
1 stalk lemon grass cut in thin slices
6 thin slices ginger
2 tablespoons fish sauce
3 tablespoons lime juice
3/4 cup coconut milk
2 chicken breast halves, without skin, cut in thin slices
1 small Thai Bird chilli, in thin slices and without seeds
2 tablespoons cilantro chopped
Salt and pepper to taste

Cook the vermicelli in hot water for 2 minutes. Strain and
set aside.
In a medium saucepan heat the broth, the lemon grass, the
ginger, the fish sauce, and the lime juice. Bring to a boil and add
the coconut milk and the chicken slices. Cook over high heat for a
few minutes until chicken is cooked; add vermicelli and the chilli.
Cook for a few seconds more; add the cilantro, and season to
taste. Serve hot.

Note: When buying canned coconut milk, be careful not to
confuse it with coconut cream for that is used when preparing
sweets.

55

five pastas

Spaghetti vongole
Makes 4 servings

5 tablespoons olive oil
1 garlic clove, minced
Fresh or dry chilli, to taste
3/4 cup peeled clam
2 cups closed clams
1/2 cup white wine
2 cups tomatoes, cut in cubes
3 tablespoons soft tomato paste
1/3 cup fresh parsley, chopped
1 teaspoon grated lemon peel
13 ounces/400 g spaghetti or linguine
Salt and pepper

Heat half the oil in a frying pan. Add the garlic, the chilli, and
cook for a few seconds. Remove chilli, if fresh, to avoid that the
sauce becomes too spicy. Add the two kinds of clams and sauté
for 1 minute. Pour white wine and let cook until clams open.
Remove all clams and set aside in a bowl; throw away any
unopened clams.
Add more oil, then the tomato and the soft tomato paste, and
simmer for a few minutes. Season to taste with salt and pepper.
Meanwhile cook the pasta in water with salt and a little olive oil
until pasta is al dente (firm to the bite). Drain and add the rest of
the olive oil. Place pasta on pan with the sauce and add clams,
the parsley, and lemon rind. Mix well and serve hot.

Note: The clams have a lot of salt and sand so they should be
thoroughly rinsed in cold water, changing water as often as
necessary. Be sure to drain them well before cooking them.

Fettuccine with mushrooms
Makes 4 servings

3 tablespoons unsalted butter
6 cups shiitake and/or mushrooms of your taste, cut in slices
1/2 cup dry white wine
$1^{1/2}$ cup whipping cream
1/2 cup chicken broth
Salt and pepper to taste
13 ounces/400 g Fettuccine
Grated Parmesan cheese

Melt butter in a frying pan, add mushrooms and sauté with a pinch of salt until they are brown on both sides. Add the wine and let cook for about 2 minutes. Fold in whipping cream and broth and cook for 7 minutes.
Meanwhile cook the fettuccine in boiling water with salt until they are al dente. Season the sauce with salt and pepper to taste and spread over the fettuccine. Serve immediately with Parmesan cheese sprinkled on top.

61

Green ravioli

Green ravioli

Makes 4 servings

Fresh green pasta
2/3 cup spinach
2 cups all-purpose flour
1/2 teaspoon salt
2 eggs
Cold water

Spinach and Ricotta filling
1 ounce/30 g unsalted butter
1/2 white onion, finely chopped
$3^{1/2}$ ounces/100 g spinach leaves
8 ounces/250 g Ricotta cheese
3 tablespoons whipping cream
Salt and pepper

Melt butter in a frying pan and add onion. Cook stirring for 5 minutes or until soft. Add the spinach and cook for 4 more minutes. Remove from heat, let stand, and chop with a knife. Fold in the ricotta, the whipping cream. Mix well and season to taste.

Sage butter
$3^{1/2}$ ounces/100 g unsalted butter
10 leaves fresh sage
Salt and pepper
Grated Parmesan cheese for serving

Melt the butter, add the sage leaves and cook for 1 minute. Remove from heat and let stand for 20 minutes. Season to taste with salt and pepper.

Cook the spinach in boiling water for 2 minutes until wilted, strain, and process to obtain a purée. Sift the flour with the salt on a flat surface or in a deep bowl and make a well in the center. Place the eggs in the well and beat with a fork; add the spinach purée and slowly fold in the flour. Add a little bit of cold water if the dough is too dry or a little more flour if the dough is too sticky until you obtain manageable dough. On well-floured surface, knead for about 4 minutes or until it is smooth and not sticky. Cover with a dry towel and let rest for about 30 minutes. Divide dough in 2 manageable portions. Roll each one with a floured rolling pin to a 1/4 inch/5 mm thickness; fold in half and roll out again. Repeat this procedure about 8 more times and roll it out again until a very thin rectangle is obtained. (If using a pasta machine, do the same by putting the dough through the device and reducing its thickness gradually until the thinnest setting has been reached.) Once you have two rectangles of pasta, distribute a small amount of filling with a rounded tablespoon three inches apart. Brush the edges and the spaces between the filling with some water and cover with the other rectangle. Press with the tips of your fingers around each filling making sure there are no air bubbles between the sheets of pasta. With a pastry wheel, trim the pasta so that the filling is in the center and 1/2 -inch/1 cm pasta stands out on the sides. Cook the ravioli in hot water with salt from 6 to 8 minutes or until they are al dente.

Drain pasta and drizzle with the sauce. Sprinkle with Parmesan cheese.

Vegetarian lasagna
Makes 8 to 10 servings

1 medium-size eggplant
1 red or yellow pepper
1 cup basil leaves
2 tablespoons olive oil
2 cups ricotta cheese
3 tablespoons whipping cream
Salt and pepper
2 portobello mushrooms
1 cup spinach, sautéed in butter
$2^{1/2}$ cups homemade tomato sauce, see page 23
1 box 14 ounces precooked lasagna
Vegetable oil and olive oil
Grated Parmesan cheese

Cut the eggplant in thin slices and place in a colander in layers, sprinkling each with salt. Let stand for 1 hour to remove sour taste. Place the pepper under the broiler at high heat. Turn until the skin blackens on all sides. The same can be done by holding the pepper on a grilling fork over a gas flame. Put it into a plastic bag and let stand. Once it is cold, peel and take out seeds; cut in fine julienne.

Heat a small amount of water and add basil leaves. Cook for 1 minute and place them in the blender. Add 1 tablespoon water in which they were cooked and the olive oil. Blend until a green liquid is obtained.

In a medium-size bowl, mix ricotta with whipping cream and basil liquid. Season with salt and pepper to taste and keep aside.

Cut the mushrooms in slices and sauté in hot olive oil in a frying pan or wok. Season with salt.

Wash the eggplant slices in cold water to remove excess salt and dry with paper towel. Brown them in vegetable oil and set aside. Preheat oven to 350° F /180° C.

Grease a 13" by 9"/32 x 23 cm glass or ceramic baking dish with butter and spread a layer of tomato sauce on the bottom. Arrange the lasagna by overlapping layers of pasta covered with ricotta mixture, the different vegetables, and tomato sauce. Finish with a ricotta layer and sprinkle Parmesan cheese on top. Bake for 20 minutes until lightly brown and serve hot.

65

Vegetarian lasagna

Farfalle with sun-dried tomatoes
Makes 4 to 6 persons

$3^{1/2}$ ounces/100 g short pasta of your taste per person
2 tablespoons olive oil
1 small white onion, chopped
1/2 cup white wine
3/4 cup dry tomatoes, rehydrated, cut in cubes
1 large can (1 pound 3 ounces/600 g) whole tomatoes, peeled
1/2 cup chicken broth
2 tablespoons capers
1 can (14 ounces/420 g) salmon
4 tablespoons flat leaf fresh parsley, chopped
2 tablespoons sugar
3 tablespoons balsamic vinegar

68

Use at least 4 quarts of water for every pound of pasta.
Add 2 teaspoons salt and a little olive oil and when the water
comes to a rapid boil, add pasta and cook until it is al dente.
In a frying pan, heat the olive oil over low heat, add the chopped
onion, and let it sweat until it is translucent. Add the white wine
and let it boil. Then add the dry tomatoes (previously rehydrated in
hot water or in olive oil), the canned tomatoes cut in cubes, the
chicken broth, and half of the capers minced. Continue cooking
until sauce has reduced and thickened slightly. Add the salmon
flaked, the rest of the capers, and the parsley. Mix well and
season with salt and pepper to taste.
In a separate saucepan, melt the sugar with the balsamic vinegar
over medium heat and cook for several minutes until you obtain a
light syrup.
Drain pasta and serve with the hot sauce and a small amount of
balsamic syrup on top.

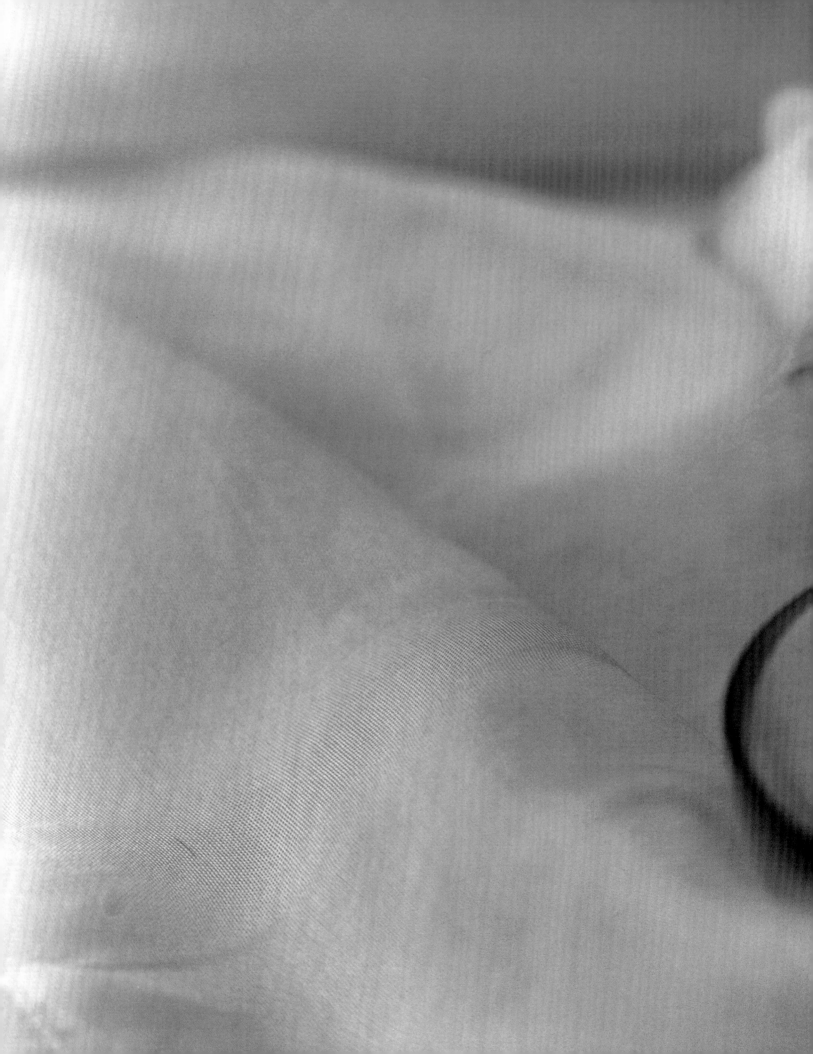

seven seafoods

Caramelized salmon

Makes 4 main-dish servings

4 pieces salmon fillets (about 4 ounces/125 g each) with skin
2 tablespoons honey
1/2 tablespoon poppy seeds
1/2 tablespoon sumak
1/2 tablespoon dry lemon
1/2 tablespoon licorice
1 ounce/30 g unsalted butter
1 tablespoon olive oil
Salt

Salmon sauce
1 tablespoon white onion, chopped
1/4 cup white wine
1 teaspoon honey
1/2 cup chicken broth
3 ounces/90 g unsalted butter
2 tablespoons lime juice

Brush salmon with honey and garnish with mixture of poppy
seeds, sumak, lemon, and licorice. Save a small quantity of
spices for the sauce. Set on a plate and chill for 1/2 hour.
Preheat oven at 350° F /180° C
Heat the olive oil in a frying pan and place salmon fillets, skin-
side down and cook for 4 minutes. Turn and cook 1 minute or
until brown. Turn again skin-side down and bake for 4 minutes
more or to taste. Avoid over cooking.
Prepare the sauce while oven is heating:
Melt some butter in a saucepan and cut the rest in cubes, keeping
it cold in the refrigerator. Add onion and sweat until translucent;
add white wine and let it evaporate for 1 minute; add honey,
chicken broth, and saved spices. Boil for 5 minutes. Reduce heat
and add lime juice and butter cubes, one by one, shaking the pan
so that the butter melts and folds in, without letting it come to a
boil. Serve inmediately when the salmon is ready.
This dish goes well with the mashed potatoes with mustard
on page 97.

Risotto nero

Risotto nero

Makes 6 servings as an entrée

8 whole squid (calamari)
2 cups fish broth
3$^{1/2}$ ounces/100 g unsalted butter
2 tablespoons olive oil
1 small onion, finely chopped
1 garlic clove, pressed and chopped
1$^{3/4}$ cups rice (arborio, vialone, nano o carnaroli)
3 envelopes squid ink pasta
3/4 cup white wine
1 tablespoon cilantro, chopped
2 to 3 tablespoons whipping cream
Salt and pepper

78

Clean the squid by holding squid body firmly in one hand, and grip head and tentacles with the other. Pull gently to remove body contents. Cut off tentacles in front of eyes. Remove and discard beak from center of tentacles. Discard head and ink sac. Pull out the clear plastic-like quill from body pocket and discard. Rub off thin dark outer skins from body and discard skin. Rinse body inside and out with cold running water; rinse tentacles also. Slice squid bodies crosswise into 3/4 inch/1.5 cm wide rings. Cut large tentacles into pieces.

Heat fish broth and bring it to a boil over high heat. Reduce heat to low and simmer covered during the preparation of the risotto. In a heavy pan with thick base, heat butter with 1 tablespoon olive oil. Sweat the chopped onion over low heat until it is soft and translucent; then over high heat, dip squid and fry for 3 minutes; add garlic and mix well.

Reduce heat to medium and add rice. Season with salt and pepper to taste. Cook, stirring; then squirt ink envelopes on top of rice and add wine; stir constantly until all the liquid is absorbed. Add about 1/2 cup simmering broth to rice mixture, stirring until liquid is absorbed. Continue cooking, adding the broth, and stirring after each addition for about 30 minutes, until all liquid is absorbed and rice is tender but still firm. Add the whipping cream and remove from heat. Note that the amount of liquid that is necessary to bring the rice to the correct tenderness may vary. In a frying pan, heat remaining olive oil and sauté the tentacles and rings. Add salt, pepper, and cilantro and serve over the risotto. This risotto also functions well with octopus.

Grilled tuna

Makes 4 servings

4 tuna fillets (about 4 ounces/125 g each)
4 tablespoons extra virgin olive oil
Salt and pepper

Hoisin and sesame sauce
2 tablespoons sesame oil
1/4 teaspoon dry chilli
1 tablespoon fresh ginger, grated
1/4 cup hoisin sauce
2 tablespoons balsamic vinegar
2 tablespoons soy sauce
2 tablespoons natural orange juice
1 teaspoon dry coriander seeds, minced

Place tuna fillets in a resealable plastic bag and add olive oil.
Seal and refrigerate for at least 1 hour.
Make sure that grill is absolutely clean to prevent tuna from
sticking. Then heat it until you can hold your hand over it for
about 2 seconds.
Take tuna out of bag and season with salt and pepper. Cook for
2 to 3 minutes on each side depending on thickness and how
you want it cooked.
Serve hot with the following sauce:
Heat oil, add chilli and ginger; cook for 2 minutes. Pour this oil in
a deep bowl and add the rest of the ingredients. Serve lukewarm
or at room temperature.

79

Grilled tuna

Ceviche

Makes 4 servings

10 ounces/300 g fresh corvina, boneless and skinless
1/4 cup cilantro, chopped
1/2 Red pepper, cut in julienne
1/4 cup red onion, finely sliced
1/4 cup chives, chopped
Juice of 2 lemons
2 tablespoons extra virgin olive oil
Salt and pepper
Chilli to taste

Cut the corvina in medium-size cubes and place them in a glass
bowl. Add cilantro, red pepper, onion, chives, and lemon juice.
Mix and refrigerate for 2 hours. Before serving, add olive oil and
season with salt, pepper, and chilli to taste. Serve with soda
crackers, toast or bread.

83

84

Shrimp dipped in crunchy coconut / Thai red fish curry

Shrimp dipped in crunchy coconut
Makes 4 servings

24 shrimp
1 cup all-purpose flour
2 eggs
2 teaspoons water
2¹/₂ cups grated coconut, dehydrated, without sugar
Salt
Vegetable oil for frying

Mango mayonnaise
1 large egg yolk
1/2 teaspoon white vinegar
3/4 cup vegetable oil
1 tablespoon lime juice
5 tablespoons mango chutney
1¹/₂ tablespoons cilantro, chopped
20 drops chili sauce or to taste

Put 1/2 cup sea salt in a deep bowl; add cold water and mix until dissolved. Place the frozen shrimp in this mixture and thaw. Shell shrimp gently and discard, leaving tail segment in place. Remove the dark vein with tip of a knife, being careful not to cut open. Rinse shrimp under cold running water. Dry well with paper towel.

Heat oil in heavy pan with thick base or deep-fry pan.

Season shrimp with salt, dredge lightly with flour; dip in beaten egg mixed with water; then coat with grated coconut. Repeat until shrimp is totally covered with coconut.

Fry the shrimp in very hot vegetable oil until they are brown and crunchy. Place on paper towel to remove excess fat and sprinkle with salt.

Serve hot with the following mayonnaise:

Place the egg yolk in a bowl and whisk with vinegar and a pinch of salt until it turns white. Add oil in a steady stream and whisk constantly until obtaining a soft, smooth mayonnaise. Fold in lemon juice, mango chutney, cilantro, salt, and chilli to taste.

Thai red fish curry

Makes 4 servings

4 tablespoons vegetable oil
1 garlic clove, chopped
2 cups wild mushrooms of your taste in thin slices
1 cup bean sprouts
3 tablespoons red curry paste
1 cup coconut milk
2 tablespoons fish sauce
2 teaspoons sugar
13 ounces/400 g firm white fish fillets, cubed
1 cup chicken broth
2 lime leaves or 2 tablespoons lime juice
3 tablespoons cilantro, chopped

Red curry paste
8 red dry chilli, without seeds, thin sliced
1 teaspoon coriander seeds
1 teaspoon white pepper
2 garlic cloves
2 lemon grass stalks, white part finely chopped
4 stalks cilantro, finely chopped
1 teaspoon grated lemon peel
1 inch piece ginger, chopped
2 teaspoons shrimp paste
1 teaspoon salt
1 tablespoon vegetable oil

In a wok or frying pan, heat half of the oil until smoke appears; add garlic and let it brown. Add mushrooms and bean sprouts and sauté for 5 minutes. Remove and save in separate dish. Pour the rest of the oil in the same wok or frying pan and heat again. Add curry paste, cook, and stir for a few seconds. Pour the coconut milk, and cook stirring until lightly thick. Add fish sauce and sugar and mix well. Then add fish and continue to cook stirring for 2 minutes. Pour chicken broth and cook for 2 more minutes. Stir in the mushrooms, bean sprouts, the lime juice or leaves and the cilantro. Serve hot.

Red curry paste:
In a food processor or mortar, mix all the ingredients until a smooth paste is obtained. If necessary, add some lukewarm water to smoothen the mixture.

87

Fresh oysters with American sauce
Makes 4 Servings

16 to 20 oysters in their shells
Ice
2 limes, cut in slices
1 cup tomato ketchup
20 drops chilli sauce or to taste
1/2 white onion, finely chopped
1/3 cup fresh parsley, chopped
2 tablespoons lime juice
2 tablespoons orange juice
2 tablespoons cognac
Salt and pepper to taste

89

Shuck oysters by carefully opening with a knife, taking care not to
spill any liquor and loosen flesh from both shells. Discard top
shell. Place over ice with lemon slices all around.
In small bowl mix ketchup, chilli, onion, parsley, lime and orange
juices, and cognac. Season with salt and pepper to taste. Serve
in a separate bowl.

five potatoes

Potatoes with caviar
Makes 4 Servings

2 cups potatoes in season
3/4 cup whipping cream
1/3 cup dry white wine
1/4 teaspoon cornstarch
Salt and pepper
1 small jar lump fish caviar
Chives, chopped

Cook the potatoes in water with salt for 15 minutes or until fork tender. Drain and cool. Meanwhile, mix cream with wine and cook over medium heat for 6 minutes. Add cornstarch previously dissolved in a little hot cream; cook over low heat, stirring for 2 minutes or until sauce begins to thicken. Remove from heat, add caviar, and season with salt and pepper to taste. Pour over potatoes and decorate with chopped chives.

93

Pommes Anna / Spanish tortilla

Pommes Anna

Makes 4 to 6 servings

10 medium-size all-purpose potatoes
4 ounces/125 g clarified butter, see page 28
Salt and pepper

Preheat oven to 425° F /220° C

Peel the potatoes and cut in fine slices with an adjustable-blade slicer (mandoline) or sharp knife. Place on paper towel and dry well. Grease a round pan with butter.

Starting with the center, cover the bottom of the pan with a layer of potatoes overlapping them slightly. Cover with some clarified butter and sprinkle with salt and pepper. Repeat this process four more times or until all the slices have been placed; last, season with salt and pepper. Cut a circle in waxed paper and cover surface of potatoes. Place in oven for 1 hour.

Remove excess fat, and let stand for 5 minutes. Loosen edge of potatoes with pancake turner; carefully invert potatoes onto warm platter. Serve hot.

Spanish tortilla

Makes 6 servings

7 medium all-purpose potatoes
1 white onion, thinly sliced
Olive oil
Sunflower oil
7 eggs
2 teaspoons salt

Peel potatoes and cut in coarsely irregular chunks and place them in a frying pan with the onion. Add enough oil (half olive and half sunflower) to cover the potatoes and the onion. Cook covered over low heat for 15 minutes or until tender (the amount of oil used, depends on the size of the pan). Uncover pan, increase heat, and fry until the edges of the potatoes begin to brown. Drain the oil and add beaten eggs with salt; return to heat and cook until brown on one side; turn over and brown on the other side. Cut in squares or triangles and serve hot or cold.

96

THE HIGH NUTRITIONAL VALUE OF THE POTATO IS LOST WHEN LEFT IN WATER FOR

TOO LONG. IT IS BETTER TO PEEL POTATOES JUST BEFORE PREPARATION.

Whipped potatoes with mustard

Makes 4 servings

8 all-purpose potatoes
3 ounces/90 g unsalted butter
1 cup whipping cream
$1^{1/2}$ tablespoons Dijon mustard or to taste
Salt and pepper

Peel potatoes and in a saucepan, heat potatoes and enough water to cover them and boil over high heat. Reduce heat to low. Cover and simmer for 15 minutes, or until fork-tender. Drain, mash with fork or potato masher and add butter and whipping cream. Stir with wooden spoon until smooth and free of lumps. Add mustard and mix well. Season with salt and pepper to taste.

Oven roasted potatoes

Makes 8 servings

8 large all- purpose potatoes
1/2 cup whipping cream
2 tablespoons whole milk
2 tablespoons unsalted butter
1/4 cup cream cheese
Salt, pepper, and nutmeg
Grated Parmesan cheese

Adjust oven rack to top level and preheat oven at 400° F/200° C. Place potatoes in baking dish and cover with aluminum foil; bake 1 hour or until a toothpick can be easily inserted in the potato and its skin feels crunchy. Remove from heat and let stand 10 minutes or until they are cold enough to manipulate. Slash tops, press to open slightly, and with a spoon take out filling, carefully leaving skin intact. Return emptied potatoes to baking dish and bake 10 minutes more, until dry and lightly toasted. Meanwhile, mash filling with a fork, add the rest of the ingredients and mix until obtaining a smooth, soft purée. Season with salt, pepper and nutmeg to taste. Remove empty potatoes from oven and increase heat to 450° F/225° C or broil. Fill potatoes with mixture and sprinkle with Parmesan cheese.
Bake for 7 minutes until surface is au gratin and brown. Serve immediately.

97

98

seven meats

Beef tenderloin with balsamic vinegar
Makes 4 servings

8 ($2^{1/2}$ ounces/70 g) beef tenderloin steaks
Olive oil
2 red onions, sliced
1/2 cup balsamic vinegar
2 small portobello mushrooms
12 stalks flat leaf or Italian parsley

Heat grill o pan with a thick base with some olive oil. Add the
onion slices and fry 3 to 4 minutes or until brown. Pour 1
teaspoon balsamic vinegar on top to caramelize lightly and turn
red. Remove and save on a plate. Then add portobello
mushrooms with a pinch of salt and fry for a few minutes until
brown. Remove and save with onions.
Seal both sides of each slice of sirloin with some olive oil and
cook on a grill or frying pan over high heat for 2 to 3 minutes on
each side or to taste. Season with salt and pepper. Meanwhile
pour the rest of the vinegar in a saucepan and let reduce for 5
minutes or until a light syrup is obtained. Remove from heat.
Alternate meat with mushrooms, onion slices, and parsley stalks
and spoon balsamic syrup over steaks.

Thai style beef with lemongrass and tamarind

Thai style beef with lemongrass and tamarind
Makes 4 to 6 servings

2 tablespoons sesame or sunflower oil
2 stalks lemongrass, finely chopped
3 shallots, cut in fine slices
1 green chilli, sliced and without seeds
1 pound 3 ounces/600 g beef tenderloin, cut in fine strips
6 tablespoons tamarind pulp
2 tablespoons fish sauce
1 tablespoon lime juice
1 tablespoon brown sugar
2 tablespoons cilantro, chopped
$1^{1/2}$ cups papaya in thick julienne
Salt

Heat oil in frying pan or wok until it smokes. Add lemon grass, shallots, and chilli, and cook for a few minutes. Add tenderloin and cook until brown on all sides; season with salt. Mix tamarind, fish sauce, lime juice, and sugar, and pour over beef. Last, add cilantro and papaya.
Serve with oriental rice on page 122.

A GOOD VEAL CUTLET SHOULD BE VERY THIN AND FREE OF MARBLING. COOK FAST,
OVER HIGH HEAT TO PRESERVE ITS FLAVORFUL JUICES AND NOT TOUGHEN

Veal skewers with black forest ham
Makes 4 servings

4 veal cutlets (4 ounces/125 g each)
16 slices black forest ham or prosciutto
28 fresh basil leaves
2 tablespoons olive oil
4 wooden skewers
1/3 cup black olives finely chopped
3 tablespoons extra virgin olive oil
Salt and pepper

To make veal evenly thick, pound with kitchen hammer, fat-side down, between two sheets of plastic wrap. Cut each escalope in four equal rectangles and place a slice of ham and a basil leaf on top. Roll each rectangle of veal so that ham is on the inside. Spear 4 veal rolls on each skewer, alternating with a basil leaf. Brush with olive oil and roast on grill or frying pan over high heat for 3 to 4 minutes on each side. Season with salt and pepper to taste. Sprinkle with black olives mixed in extra virgin olive oil and serve.

Veal skewers with black forest ham

Mustard-crusted steak

Makes 4 servings

4 beef tenderloin steaks (7 ounces/200 g each)
2 tablespoons vegetable oil
6 tablespoons mustard seeds
1 ounce/30 g unsalted butter
2 tablespoons Cognac
1/3 cup white wine
2 tablespoons Dijon mustard
1/2 cup whipping cream
Salt and pepper

Brush each steak on both sides with oil and press mustard seeds
on top so they stick well to meat. Melt butter in a large frying pan
and cook steaks from 2 to 4 minutes on each side until desired
doneness.

Add Cognac and flambé (making sure the stove extractor is not
on). Remove from heat, and place steaks on a rack and let stand.
Meanwhile add wine and let it evaporate, stirring to gather all
meat juices and brown bits are loosened. Stir in mustard and
whipping cream, and cook for 2 minutes. Season with salt and
pepper to taste and serve immediately.

111

Pork tenderloin with cinnamon / Pork chops in prune sauce

Pork tenderloin with cinnamon
Makes 6 to 8 servings

1 or 2 pork tenderloins, total weight 3 pounds/1500 g
2 cloves per tenderloin
Salt and pepper
1/4 cup ground cinnamon
2 tablespoons olive oil
1 star anise
5 juniper berries

Calvados sauce
1/2 cup Calvados
1/2 cup dry white wine
3/4 cup chicken broth
1 teaspoon all-purpose flour
2 tablespoons unsalted butter, cut in cubes

Glazed shallots
24 Shallots
water
1 ounce/30 g unsalted butter
1 pinch salt
1 tablespoon sugar

Peel shallots keeping them whole and place them in a saucepan.
Cover with water, salt, and sugar. Then cover with parchment
paper and boil over medium heat until onions are tender and
water has evaporated completely. Shake pan so that onions
brown lightly and glaze turning brilliant and caramelized.

Trim excess fat from pork before cooking. Insert cloves in
tenderloin. Season with salt and pepper, and brush well with
cinnamon. Melt butter in a large frying pan and add oil. Place
tenderloin and the other spices. Brown on all sides and continue
cooking over medium heat until it is cooked. Remove from heat
and let stand on rack for at least 10 minutes before cutting.
Remove excess fat from frying pan and pour in Calvados,
flambé, and cook for 1 minute. Add wine and boil.
Then add chicken broth; let reduce for a few minutes, and
add flour previously dissolved in some of this liquid and mix
well. Once it starts to thicken, add butter very cold, stirring
until blended in. Do not let it boil.
Strain and serve hot with sliced tenderloin with the following
glazed onions and apples sautéd with Calvados on page 179.

114

Pork chops in prune sauce

Makes 4 servings

4 pork loin chops

Prune sauce
1 tablespoon unsalted butter
1 small white onion, finely chopped
1 cup pitted prunes
3/4 cup dry white wine
1 cup chicken broth
1 cup whipping cream
Sunflower oil

In a frying pan, sear chops on both sides with some oil and cook over high heat for 6 minutes on each side (depending on thickness of chops) or until meat thermometer registers 160° F/80° C. Serve with prune sauce poured over chops.

Prune sauce:
Melt butter in a saucepan, add onion, and sweat over low heat for 6 minutes or until translucent. Meanwhile, in a separate saucepan, boil prunes with wine for 5 minutes and let stand. Drain over the onion, add 5 prunes, and save the rest. Then add chicken broth, and let reduce for 5 minutes over high heat. Add cream, the remaining prunes, salt to taste, and cook for 5 more minutes. Remove from heat.

115

Veal wrapped in bacon
Makes 4 servings

4 veal tenderloins
Salt and pepper
8 slices smoked bacon
12 fresh oregano leaves
Wooden toothpicks
1 teaspoon olive oil
1 tablespoon white onion, chopped
1/4 cup white wine
1/2 cup chicken broth
2 tablespoons teriyaki sauce
1 tablespoon Worcester sauce
1 teaspoon soy sauce
1 ounce/30 g unsalted butter, very cold
olive oil (for frying veal)

Season veal tenderloins with salt and pepper and wrap each in
bacon slices and oregano leaves, securing them with toothpicks.
In a saucepan, add olive oil and sweat onion until trasnlucent;
add wine and let it evaporate; add broth, teriyaki sauce,
Worcester sauce, and soy sauce; let reduce to half the amount.
Last, add butter shaking pan so it blends together. Remove
from heat.
Heat frying pan slightly covered with olive oil and add veal
tenderloins. Brown on all sides and bake for five minutes or until
cooked to taste. Serve immediately with the hot sauce poured
over veal tenderloins.

116

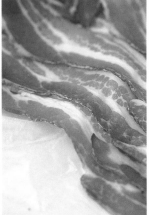

four rice dishes

Scented Jasmine rice with coconut
Makes 4 servings

1 cup Jasmine rice
1 cup coconut milk
3/4 cup water
1/2 teaspoon salt

Wash rice until water is clear to wash away starchy coating. Pour coconut milk and water into a heavy pan with thick base and add rice, salt, and let boil. Stir with wooden spoon until water is absorbed. Cover and seal tight, and continue cooking over low heat for 20 minutes. Remove from heat and let stand. Fluff lightly with a fork and serve hot.
It you don't want rice scented with coconut, just prepare as follows:

Plain rice
Makes 4 servings
1 cup jasmine rice
1 3/4 cups water
Salt (optional)

Wash rice until water is completely clear. Pour water in heavy pan with thick base and add rice, (salt) and let boil. Stir with wooden spoon until water is absorbed. Cover and seal tight, and continue cooking over low heat for 20 minutes. Remove from heat and let stand. Fluff lightly with fork and serve hot.

122

Risotto with wild mushrooms and blue cheese

Risotto with wild mushrooms and blue cheese

Makes 2 generous servings

4 tablespoons unsalted butter
1/2 white onion, chopped
4 fresh shiitake and/or mushrooms of your taste, sliced
1/4 cup dry white wine
3 cups chicken or vegetable broth
1 cup Arborio rice
2 ounces/60 g blue cheese
Salt and pepper to taste
2 tablespoons fresh parsley chopped

In a heavy pan with thick base, melt some butter, and cook onion until translucent. Meanwhile, in a separate frying pan, sauté mushrooms with the rest of butter until brown; add pinch of salt and cook for 2 more minutes. Then add wine and let it evaporate for 2 minutes; remove from heat. Blend 1 cup sautéd mushrooms with broth in blender until a smooth mixture is obtained, and save the rest.

Once onion is tender, add rice. Add some mushroom broth very hot and cook stirring with a wooden spoon until it begins to dry. Repeat this process adding liquid and stirring for approximately 25 minutes or until rice is al dente. You might not need all the liquid. Last, add blue cheese in small chunks and mix well. Season with salt and pepper to taste; add fresh parsley and serve immediately.

126

Wild rice with cranberries
Makes 8 servings

1 1/2 cups wild rice
3 cups chicken or vegetable broth
2 cups water
1/2 teaspoon salt
3 tablespoons sunflower oil
1 stalk scallion
2 cups white short-grain rice
4 cups water
3/4 teaspoon salt
3/4 cup dried cranberries

Rinse wild rice until water is clear and place in saucepan. Add broth, water, and salt; boil for 40 to 45 minutes or until tender and some grains start to separate on the edges.

In a separate saucepan, pour oil and fry onion lightly for 1 minute. Add rinsed white rice and 3 cups water. Stir and let dry; add remaining cup of water mixed with salt, and fluff lightly with a fork and let dry again. Cover with aluminum foil, cook covered over low heat for 20 minutes or until grain is tender and fluffy. Remove from heat and let stand for 10 minutes.

Mix the two types of rice, add cranberries, and gently stir until blended. Serve hot.

127

Wild rice with cranberries

Rice with coconut
Makes 6 to 8 servings

2 small coconuts
Water
1 cup Coca-cola
1/2 teaspoon brown sugarloaf tincture
3/4 teaspoon salt
1$^{1/2}$ teaspoons sugar
1/2 cup hot water
2/3 cup raisins
2 cups short-grain white rice

Take out water from coconuts and pour into measuring cup. Add water until you have 3 cups. Add Coca-cola, tincture, salt, sugar and save.

Peel coconuts and cut in small chunks. Place them in blender, add hot water and blend to extract coconut milk. Pour into heavy pan with thick base and cook over medium heat for 10 minutes or until coconut oil separates and begins to form cracklings.

Add raisins, rice, and the mixture of liquids. Reduce to low heat, cover and seal tight; cook for 25 minutes or until rice grains separate easily. Remove from heat, let stand a few minutes, fluff with a fork and serve hot.

131

three chickens

Baked chicken with tangerine

Makes 4 servings

1 whole chicken
3 tablespoons unsalted butter
2 tablespoons ground cinnamon
Salt and pepper
2 tangerines
4 stalks peppermint or fresh mint
2 sticks cinnamon
1 orange
$1^{1/2}$ cups orange juice
1/4 cup port

134

Preheat oven at 350° F / 180° C.
Rinse chicken inside and out until water comes out clear. Pat dry
with paper towels.
Stir butter at room temperature with ground cinnamon. Carefully
push fingers between skin and meat to loosen skin in the neck
cavity and spread half of the mixture of butter and cinnamon
underneath. Coat the surface with the rest of the mixture and
sprinkle with salt.
Cut tangerines in half, squeeze their juice over chicken inside and
out. Stuff chicken with tangerine rinds, half of the mint leaves, and
1 cinnamon stick. Roast chicken on a rack in a roasting pan
resting on one of its wings, placing orange sliced in quarters, the
rest of the mint leaves, and a cinnamon stick.
Roast for 1 hour turning it so that it cooks 15 minutes on each
side and the rest on its back, basting it occasionally with orange
juice. Once chicken is brown and thoroughly cooked, pour the
port over the chicken. Remove from heat, cut, and serve with
cooked juices.

Chicken satays with peanut sauce

Chicken satays with peanut sauce
Makes 12 to 14 servings

1 teaspoon coriander seeds
4 chicken breast fillets
2 tablespoons light soy sauce
1 teaspoon salt
4 tablespoons vegetable oil
1 tablespoon curry powder (Oriental)
1 tablespoon turmeric
8 tablespoons coconut milk
12 to 14 wooden skewers

Peanut sauce
2 tablespoons vegetable oil
1 garlic clove, chopped
1 tablespoon red curry paste, see page 87.
8 tablespoons coconut milk
3/4 cup chicken broth
1 tablespoon sugar
1 teaspoon salt
1 tablespoon lime juice
4 tablespoons peanuts, toasted and crushed or peanut butter
2 tablespoons breadcrumbs

138

In a frying pan over medium heat, place coriander seeds stirring for 5 minutes without letting them brown. Remove from heat and crush.
Cut fillets in thin slices lengthwise, calculating to obtain between 24 and 28 slices, depending on size of the fillets. Add all the ingredients, and let marinate in the refrigerator for at least 1 hour. Heat grill, frying pan or barbecue.
Skewer the chicken strips by folding them back and forth as if sewing through them. Fry until chicken is well cooked and brown on both sides. Serve with the following peanut sauce:

In a frying pan, heat oil until smoke appears. Add garlic and let it brown. Then add curry paste and mix well. Stir in coconut milk and cook for a few seconds. Add broth, sugar, salt, and lime juice; cook for 2 minutes stirring constantly. Last, add peanuts and breadcrumbs and fold in well.

Chicken burgers
Makes 6 servings

1 pound 3 ounces/600 g chicken breasts
1 tablespoon unsalted butter
1/2 white onion, finely chopped
1 egg
1 tablespoon sweet chilli sauce
2 tablespoons cilantro, chopped
1/4 cup breadcrumbs
Salt and pepper to taste
1/4 cup sesame oil
Bread, lettuce and tomato of your choice to serve

Lime and sweet chilli sauce
1/2 cup mayonnaise
2 tablespoons sweet chilli sauce
1/2 tablespoon lime juice

With the help of a grinder or food processor, grind the chicken meat. Heat butter in a saucepan, add onion, and sweat over low heat until it is translucent. Remove from heat and let stand. Place ground chicken in a bowl, add egg and onion, and mix with thoroughly. Add chilli sauce, cilantro, and breadcrumbs, and fold in well. Season with salt and pepper. The mixture should feel sticky when touched. Grease your hands with some sesame oil to allow easier shaping of burger patties. Divide mixture into 6 equal portions, and then shape patties.
Preheat oven to 350° F/180° C.
Heat frying pan with remaining oil and cook burgers for 6 minutes on each side. Place in oven, and cook for 10 more minutes. If desired, cook on grill or frying pan over low heat to avoid burning before the inside is cooked.
Serve with bread, lettuce and tomato or vegetables of your taste with the following sauce:
Mix mayonnaise with chilli sauce and lime juice. Add salt and pepper to taste.

139

140

Chicken burgers

one pizza

144

Pizza with artichokes and Manchego cheese

Pizza with artichokes and Manchego cheese
12–inch/30 cm diameter

Pizza dough
1 teaspoon sugar
1 teaspoon dry active yeast
1/3 cup lukewarm water
1 tablespoon lukewarm whole milk
8 ounces/250 g all-purpose flour
1/2 teaspoon salt
2 tablespoons olive oil

Basic pizza sauce
4 red tomatoes, peeled
3 leaves fresh basil
1 tablespoon tomato paste
$1^{1/2}$ tablespoons extra virgin olive oil
Salt and pepper

146

Put sugar and yeast in a bowl; add water and milk and mix to let the yeast activate. In a separate bowl, mix flour with salt and oil, add yeast mixture, and fold in. Turn onto lightly floured surface and knead 5 minutes or until smooth, and dough comes away from hands.

Brush the inside of a large bowl lightly with olive oil, shape dough into a ball, and place it in the bowl. With a knife, trace a cross on the surface and let it rest in a warm area for 1 hour or until it has doubled in size.

Preheat oven to 475° F/240° C.

Pound dough with your hands until it goes back to its original size. Turn onto lightly floured surface and shape with fingertips to form a circle about 12 inch/30 cm in diameter, bringing edges of dough up; fold to make a 1-inch/2.5 cm rim. Place dough in a metal round pan lightly greased with oil. Cover with the following sauce and topping:

Blend peeled tomatoes with basil, tomato paste, and olive oil. Season to taste with salt and pepper, and spread over pizza dough.

Manchego cheese pizza topping
3 ounces/90 g Manchego cheese, grated
2 ounces/60 g Mozzarella cheese, grated
1 large red tomato, sliced
1/4 cup fresh basil leaves
4 marinated artichoke hearts, cut in quarters
1/2 teaspoon dry chilli flakes
1 tablespoon olive oil
Ground black pepper

Spread grated cheese evenly to cover entire dough surface. Then
arrange tomato slices, basil leaves, artichoke hearts, and chilli.
Sprinkle with olive oil and pepper. Bake for 15 minutes or until
brown. In locations near the sea, this sauce should not boil
because it will separate immediately. In high altitudes, it can boil
briefly until the desired thickness is reached.

five sauces

Bernaise sauce

Makes 1 cup

1 tablespoon white onion, finely chopped
1 tablespoon dry tarragon
3 tablespoons vinegar or white wine
2 egg yolks
2 tablespoons cold water
4 ounces/125 g unsalted butter
Salt and pepper to taste

Place onion, tarragon, and vinegar or white wine in a saucepan, and cook over medium heat until liquid has evaporated completely, and the ingredients begin to stick to bottom of pan. Add egg yolks well beaten with water and whisk in a Bain Marie (double boiler or water bath) until mixture thickens like a mayonnaise.
Without stopping to whisk, add soft butter in cubes until completely folded in. Season with salt and pepper to taste and serve immediately.

152

Spicy tomato and Brie sauce
Makes 4 servings

5 ounces/150 g bacon
1 tablespoon olive oil
1/2 pearl onion, finely chopped
1 garlic clove, crushed
1/3 cup white wine
1 pound 3 ounces/600 g fresh or canned red tomatoes
1 cup white mushrooms, cut in quarters and sautéd in butter
1/2 cup black or green olives, seedless and sliced
1 tablespoon capers, chopped
2$^{1/2}$ ounces/70 g Brie cheese, in small chunks
1/4 teaspoon dry chilli flakes
1/4 cup whipping cream
3 tablespoons flat parsley, chopped
Salt and pepper

Heat a frying or saucepan, add bacon and cook until crisp.
Drain on paper towel and chop finely. Discard excess fat and
without rinsing, add olive oil and onion; cook over low heat for 5
minutes or until tender and translucent. Add garlic and wine and
let it evaporate. Then add peeled and chopped tomatoes.
Season with salt and pepper, and over medium heat, cook for 15
minutes or until sauce thickens or darkens.
Before serving, add mushrooms, olives, capers, brie, chilli, and
whipping cream, stirring until all ingredients have folded in. Last,
add parsley and chopped bacon. Serve hot over boneless grilled
chicken breasts or with long pasta of your taste.

Note: When peeling a garlic clove, cut it in a half lengthwise and
remove any bitter tasting green core as it will cause indigestion.

156

Mango and ginger chutney / Caramel Sauce

Mango and ginger chutney

Makes 2 cups

3 large mangos, peeled and cut in cubes
3/4 cup brown sugar
1/2 cup white raisins
1/2 white onion, finely chopped
$1^{1/2}$ tablespoons crystallized ginger
1 teaspoon lime juice
1 teaspoon curry powder
1/4 teaspoon salt

Mix all the ingredients in a saucepan. Boil over medium heat, cover, and stir occasionally for 30 minutes or until most of the liquid is absorbed. Let stand and store in sterilized jars for up to three weeks in the refrigerator.

158

Caramel sauce
Makes 1$^{3/4}$ cups

1 cup water
2 cups sugar
1$^{1/4}$ cups whipping cream
1 pinch salt
3 tablespoons unsalted butter

In a saucepan, pour water and sugar, and cook over high heat for 15 minutes or until a light caramel is formed. Reduce heat and simmer for a few more minutes until caramel turns amber color. Meanwhile, in another saucepan, bring cream with salt to a boil and slowly add to the caramel that was removed from the heat; make sure all bubbles disappear before adding more. Last, fold in butter, let stand for a few minutes, and serve.

159

Crème anglaise

Makes 1 cup

1 $^{1/4}$ cups whole milk
1 tablespoon vanilla extract (or flavor of your taste)
2 egg yolks
2 tablespoons sugar

In a double boiler, bring milk to a boil with vanilla. In a separate bowl whisk egg yolks with sugar until smooth and lemon-colored. Pour over hot milk and blend well. Cook over medium heat, stirring constantly with a wooden spoon until mixture thickens slightly and coats back of spoon well. (A finger run across the custard-coated spoon should leave a track known as nappé consistency.) Remove from heat and strain into a clean bowl placed over a larger bowl with ice to help reduce its temperature in a shorter period of time.

160

three berries

Champagne gelatin with berries

Makes 8 to 10 servings

2 tablespoons unflavored gelatin
1/2 cup water
$3^{1/2}$ cups champagne or sparkling white wine
1 cup sugar
1 tablespoon rose water
3 cups strawberries, cut in quarters
$1^{1/2}$ cups blueberries
Mint leaves (optional)

164

Sprinkle unflavored gelatin uniformly over the water, and let stand
for 5 minutes.
Heat half of the champagne or wine in a saucepan; add sugar,
and dissolve. Remove from heat. Then add gelatin, and stir until
gelatin is completely dissolved. Combine with the rest of the
champagne or wine and rose water.
Distribute the fruit into 8 to 10 champagne glasses, cover with
liquid gelatin, and refrigerate for at least 2 hours.
Serve cold and decorate with mint leaves if so desired.
Do not use raspberries or blackberries for they will bleed.

Panna cotta with strawberry and rose sauce

Panna cotta with strawberry and rose sauce

Makes 8 to 10 servings

1 cup whole milk
$2^{3/4}$ teaspoons unflavored gelatin
$2^{1/2}$ cups heavy or whipping cream
1 3-inch vanilla bean/or 1/2 tablespoon vanilla extract
7 tablespoons sugar
1 pinch salt

Strawberry and rose sauce
1/2 cup water
1/2 cup sugar
3 tablespoons rose water

2 cups fresh strawberries, hulled and cut in half
Fresh strawberries cut in quarters and mint leaves for decoration (optional)

168

Pour the milk into a medium-size saucepan and sprinkle unflavored gelatin uniformly over it. Let stand for 10 minutes. Meanwhile put ice cubes and cold water in a large bowl and pour the cream into another bowl that will fit inside.
Cut vanilla bean lengthwise iand scrape out the seeds. Stir them into the cream and add the vanilla extract.
Heat milk over high heat until gelatin is completely dissolved but do not boil. Remove from heat, add sugar and salt and stir to dissolve. In one steady stream, pour cream into the milk, stirring constantly. Return the mixture into the bowl and place over ice cubes and water. Stir frequently for 10 minutes or just until the mixture begins to mound when dropped from a spatula.
Immediately remove from ice bath and strain into a pitcher. Distribute into eight or ten ramekins or wine glasses. Cover with plastic wrap, taking care not to let the plastic touch the contents. Refrigerate for at least 4 hours.
Panna cotta can be served in the ramekins or glasses or be unmolded by submerging them in hot water for a few seconds. Tapping the sides of ramekins sharply will help to break the seal. Invert each onto a dessert plate.
Serve with the following sauce:
Boil the water and sugar over high heat until a syrup forms. Remove from heat, add 2 tablespoons rose water, and let stand. Place strawberries in a separate saucepan, add the syrup and cook for 10 minutes. Remove from heat, blend the sauce and let stand until cool. Add the remaining rose water. Spoon some sauce around each panna cotta and garnish with remaining strawberries and mint leaves if desired.

Tiramisu with red fruit
Makes 8 to 10 servings

1 cup blackberries
1/2 cup water
1/4 cup sugar
1/4 cup water
1/2 cup sugar
1/2 cup crème de Cassis
3 cups red fruit (cherries, raspberries, and blackberries)
4 egg yolks
1/2 cup sugar
7 ounces/200 g Mascarpone cheese
4 egg whites
30 ladyfingers
Sliced almonds, toasted, for decorating

Place blackberries in a saucepan with 1/2 cup water and 1/4 cup sugar. Cook over medium heat for 10 minutes. Remove from heat, blend, and reserve.

Place remaining water and sugar in a saucepan, and cook over high heat until a light caramel is obtained. Add Cassis and cook until sugar dissolves again. Add fruit, cut in halves, and the previously prepared blackberry sauce and simmer for 5 minutes. Remove from heat and let stand.

Whisk egg yolks with sugar until creamy. Add mascarpone and fold in completely, In separate bowl, beat egg whites to soft peaks, and with a rubber spatula, gently fold in to the mixture of mascarpone.

Spread enough ladyfingers with the fruit sauce to cover the bottom of a 10-inch/25 cm dish. Cover with fruit, and then with a layer of cheese mixture. Repeat process until there are two layers of ladyfingers, ending with mascarpone. Refrigerate for several hours or over night.

Decorate with sliced almonds lightly toasted and serve very cold.

169

170

Tiramisu with red fruit

five apples and cinnamon

Crème brûlée with cinnamon
Makes 6 servings

2 cups whipping cream
3/4 cup whole milk
1/2 cup sugar
1 tablespoon ground cinnamon
4 egg yolks
1 egg
1/2 cup brown sugar

Preheat oven to 250° F/120° C.

In a saucepan pour cream, milk, half the sugar, and cinnamon, and bring to a boil.

Meanwhile mix the rest of the sugar with the egg yolks, and the egg. Strain over the hot milk mixture and stir well. Pour into small ramekins or one large ceramic dish, and set in a large roasting pan with two paper towels underneath. Place on oven rack, and fill pan with boiling water to come halfway up side of dish. Cook for $1^{1/2}$ hours or until it is firm in the center. Remove from oven, let stand, and refrigerate. Just before serving, sprinkle surface with brown sugar and caramelize in oven at broil or with kitchen torch. Serve immediately.

174

Tarte Tatin / Apples sautéed in Calvados

Tarte tatin

Makes 6 to 8 servings

8 medium-size apples (Granny Smith)
2 ounces/60 g unsalted butter
3/4 cup sugar
Tart pastry

Tart pastry
1³/⁴ cups all-purpose flour
1 pinch salt
5 ounces/150 g cold unsalted butter, cut in cubes
1 egg yolk

178

Place the butter and sugar in a 10-inch/25 cm cast iron or stainless steel frying pan. Do not use a teflon-coated pan. Heat until butter and sugar have melted. Fan apples one by one tightly until surface is completely covered. Cook over low heat for 35 to 40 minutes or until apples are tender, caramel is of amber color, and excess liquid has evaporated. With a pastry brush, spread caramel often to caramelize apples on both sides. Preheat oven to 375° F/190° C.

Sift flour with salt in a bowl; add butter in cubes, and rub with fingertips until mixture looks like breadcrumbs. Add egg yolk and some water (2 to 3 teaspoons), and mix until dough begins to blend and becomes consistent. Shape into a ball and wrap in plastic. Let stand in the refrigerator for half an hour.
With rolling pin, roll dough over flat, lightly floured surface. Place dough over apples, and push edges inside pan. Bake 25 to 30 minutes or until dough is cooked. Remove from oven and let stand for 5 minutes before turning over on a serving plate.

Apples sautéed in Calvados
Makes 6 to 8 servings

6 apples
3 ounces/90 g unsalted butter
1 tablespoon sugar
1/4 cup Calvados
1/4 cup orange juice (optional)
1 tablespoon grated orange rind
Salt and pepper

Peel the apples and cut into 6 or 8 slices. Melt butter in frying or saucepan and sauté apples over high heat until lightly brown. Lower heat to medium, add sugar, and cook for 10 minutes or until apples are cooked, though not tender. Add Calvados and flambé. Pour juice and rind, and let boil. Remove from heat and season with salt and pepper to taste. Serve hot.

This can be served with pork tenderloin with cinnamon on page 114.

179

Apple crumble

Apple crumble
Makes 6 servings

6 apples
2 ounces/60 g unsalted butter
1/2 cup sugar
1 teaspoon vanilla extract
1 teaspoon ground cinnamon
1 lime (optional)

Apple crumble dough
1 cup all-purpose flour
1/4 cup sugar
1/2 teaspoon salt
1/2 teaspoon ground cinnamon
1/4 teaspoon nutmeg
3$^{1/2}$ ounces/100 g unsalted butter, cut in cubes

182

Peel apples, remove cores, and cut in quarters. In a frying pan melt butter, add sugar, vanilla, and cinnamon and sauté until brown on both sides.

In a separate bowl, mix flour, sugar, salt, cinnamon, and nutmeg. Then add cold butter, and rub with fingertips until having breadcrumb consistency. Save in refrigerator until ready to use. Preheat oven to 375° F/190° C.

Place apples in a baking dish, and sprinkle with breadcrumbs. Bake for 15 to 20 minutes or until brown on top. Serve hot or at room temperature with vanilla ice cream or whipped cream.

Apple cake with cinnamon
Makes 10 to 12 servings

2 tablespoons unsalted butter

4 tablespoons sugar

4 tablespoons brown sugar

3 eggs

2 egg yolks

1/2 cup sour cream

1 tablespoon Calvados

2$^{1/4}$ cups all-purpose flour

1 cup sugar

2 teaspoons baking powder

1 pinch salt

1 teaspoon ground cinnamon

8 ounces/250 g unsalted butter, cold and cut in cubes

2 apples (Granny Smith), peeled and cut into cubes

2 tablespoons brown sugar

1/2 teaspoon ground cinnamon

Whipped cream

1 cup whipping cream

1 teaspoon confectioner's sugar

1/2 teaspoon vanilla extract

Adjust baking rack to middle level and preheat oven to 350° F/180° C.

Greyase non-sticking *Bundt* style pan. Sprinkle sugar to cover all edges of pan and spread the rest on bottom of pan. Add brown sugar to the bottom.

In a separate bowl, whisk eggs and egg yolk, and fold in sour cream and Calvados.

In deep bowl, mix flour, sugar, baking powder, salt, and cinnamon. With an electric mixer, blend the butter in until it has a sandy consistency. Add 1/2 cup of the creamy mixture, and beat at low speed for a few seconds. Then increase speed, and continue beating until mixture is tender and creamy. Without stopping to beat, add the rest of the liquid in one steady stream until completely folded in.

Mix apples in cubes with brown sugar and cinnamon, and distribute on bottom of pan. Spread dough over surface with a plastic spatula. Bake for 45 minutes or until a toothpick inserted in the center comes out clean.

Remove from oven and turn out on rack previously covered with aluminum foil. Let stand for 1 hour. Sprinkle with confectioner's sugar (optional) and serve with whipped cream.

To prepare whipped cream, put all the ingredients in a cold bowl and whisk until it forms soft peaks. Serve hot or at room temperature.

If some pieces of the caramelized apples stick to bottom of pan, detach carefully and return to their original place in the cake, while still hot.

183

184

Apple cake with cinnamon

seven chocolates

Chocolate mousse
Makes 6 to 8 servings

7 ounces/200 g dark semisweet chocolate
4 tablespoons unsalted butter
1 pinch salt
1 teaspoon vanilla extract (optional)
2$^{1/2}$ tablespoons Grand Marnier, Cointreau, Cognac, Brandy
or black coffee
4 egg yolks
4 egg whites
2 tablespoons sugar
1 cup whipping cream

190

In a deep bowl in a Bain Marie (double boiler or water bath) or
in microwave oven melt chocolate with butter. Add salt, vanilla,
and liqueur of your taste; mix until smooth. Add egg yolks one by
one and set aside.

Place egg whites in a bowl within another bowl with hot water
until egg whites are lukewarm. Beat with hand mixer until soft
peaks form; add sugar slowly and continue beating until whites
stand in stiff, glossy peaks.

Mix 1/4 of the whites mixture with the chocolate, and fold in the
rest gently in with a plastic spatula.

Whisk whipping cream until wrinkles form, and fold in gently with
the mousse.

Pour into individual ramekins or a large one, cover with plastic
wrap, and refrigerate for at least 3 hours.

Cold lime soufflé with white chocolate

Cold lime soufflé with white chocolate

Makes 8 servings

1/2 cup lime juice
$2^{1/2}$ teaspoons unflavored gelatin
1 cup whole milk
3/4 cup sugar
2 egg yolks
1/4 teaspoon cornstarch
2 ounces/60 g white chocolate, chopped
$2^{1/2}$ teaspoons grated lemon rind
5 egg whites
3/4 cup whipping cream
2 ounces/60 g white chocolate, grated

194

Place lime juice in a deep bowl and sprinkle gelatin in a uniform layer. Set aside.

Heat milk with half the sugar in a saucepan and stir occasionally until it boils and sugar dissolves.

Meanwhile beat egg yolks with remaining sugar and cornstarch until pale and creamy. Add hot milk in a steady stream without stopping to stir. Return to stove, and over low heat, cook until mixture thickens lightly. Strain into a clean bowl, add chopped chocolate, and fold in. Then add lime and gelatin, lemon rind, and mix well. Place in a large bowl filled with water and ice and let stand.

Meanwhile beat egg whites until soft peaks forms and add the other half of sugar little by little. Mix 1/3 egg whites with lime mixture, and fold in the rest gently with a plastic spatula. Whisk cream in the same bowl of the egg whites until soft wrinkles appear and fold in gently to the soufflé. Pour into a ceramic dish and chill for $1^{1/2}$ hours. Decorate with grated chocolate and serve very cold.

Chocoflan
Makes 8 to 10 servings

Crème caramel
1 large can condensed milk
1/2 cup water, warm
4 large eggs

Caramel garnish
1/2 cup sugar
water

Chocolate torte
$3^{1/2}$ ounces/100 g unsalted butter cut in small squares
$2^{1/2}$ ounces/70 g sugar
2 egg yolks
2 ounces/60 g all-purpose flour
1 ounce/30 g unsweetened cocoa
1 teaspoon baking powder
1 teaspoon vanilla extract
4 tablespoons water one by one
2 egg whites

Preheat oven to 350° F/180° C
In a small saucepan over low heat, mix the condensed milk with the water, and add the eggs, one at the time until well mixed.
In a separate saucepan over medium heat, heat 1/2 cup sugar with sufficient water to moisten the sugar until melted. It will need to acquire a light caramel color by stirring constantly for about 5 minutes. Immediately pour into one 10-inch/25 cm ovenproof ramekin turning it so that the caramel covers the bottom.
In a large bowl, with wire whisk or fork, mix the butter with the sugar until creamy. Beat the egg yolks one by one until well blended. Beat in flour, unsweetened cocoa, and baking powder. Then beat in the vanilla extract and water until well mixed.
In a separate bowl beat the egg whites with a mixer at high speed until soft peaks form. With rubber spatula, carefully fold in with the chocolate mixture.
Pour the crème caramel into the caramelized ramekin making sure there are no bubbles; then pour the chocolate mixture lightly and spread with a wooden spatula until the surface is completely covered.
Place the ramekin in a large roasting pan on paper towels or in a Bain Marie; place pan in the oven in the middle rack. Carefully add boiling water until it comes halfway up the side of the ramekin. Bake for one hour or until Chocoflan has settled, and a knife inserted in center of custard comes out clean. Remove ramekin from water in roasting pan and let it stand until cold. Invert Chocoflan onto a dessert plate. Chill until served.

Begin 3 hours before serving or early in the day

195

196

Three chocolate brownies
Makes 16

3 ounces/90 g semisweet chocolate
3 ounces/90 g milk chocolate
5 ounces/150 g unsalted butter
3 tablespoons unsweetened cocoa
3 eggs
1$^{1/4}$ cups sugar
2 teaspoons vanilla extract
1/2 teaspoon salt
1 cup all-purpose flour
1/2 teaspoon baking powder
2/3 cup white chocolate, chopped

Preheat oven at 350° F/180° C.
Cover a metal baking pan (9" by 9"/20 x 20 cm) with two sheets of aluminum foil with edges sticking out. Lightly grease foil with butter or pan coating spray. Melt the two chocolates with butter in a Bain Marie (double boiler or water bath) or in a microwave oven and let stand. Add cocoa.
On a separate bowl, whisk eggs with sugar, vanilla, and salt, and fold in with the chocolate mixture. Add sifted flour with baking powder and last, fold in white chocolate.
Bake 45 minutes, remove from heat, and let stand for 2 hours or until cool. Cut brownies lengthwise into four strips and crosswise into 4 pieces.

199

Pears with port and chocolate fudge / Chocolate fondant

Pears with port and chocolate fudge
Makes 4 servings

2 cups water
1 cup sugar
4 pears, peeled
1/2 cup port

Chocolate fudge
5 ounces/150 g dark semisweet chocolate
1/4 cup unsweetened cocoa
1/3 cup water
1/4 cup sugar
1/2 cup corn syrup
1/4 cup whipping cream
1 teaspoon vanilla extract
1 pinch salt
2 tablespoons unsalted butter

In a saucepan, boil water and sugar until dissolved. Add pears, cover, and simmer for 25 minutes or until tender. Add port, uncover, and let evaporate turning pan at the end so the pears caramelize on all sides. Serve on dessert plate, and cover with the following hot chocolate fudge.

Melt chocolate in a Bain Marie (double boiler or water bath). Remove from heat, and fold in cocoa. Meanwhile, in a saucepan mix water and sugar, corn syrup, and whipping cream. Over medium heat, bring to a boil and simmer for 4 minutes. Remove from heat, and add vanilla, salt, and butter. Fold in melted chocolate. Makes 1 cup

202

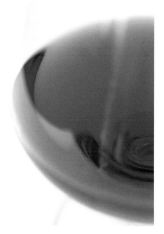

Chocolate fondant

Makes 6 servings

Butter and flour for ramekins
4 eggs
1 egg yolk
1 teaspoon vanilla extract
1/4 teaspoon salt
1/2 cup sugar
7 ounces/200 g semisweet chocolate
4 ounces/125 g unsalted butter
2 tablespoons all-purpose flour
Cocoa or confectioner's sugar to decorate

Adjust oven rack in the center and preheat oven to 400° F/200° C.

Grease and flour 6 small oven safe ramekins. Beat eggs, egg yolk, vanilla, salt, and sugar with an electric mixer until mixture is three times its original size and has a thick, pale, creamy consistency. Meanwhile melt the chocolate with butter in a Bain Marie (double boiler or water bath) or in a microwave oven. Sprinkle flour over egg mixture and lightly fold in the melted chocolate. Fill ramekins 1/2 inch/1 cm below the edge, and bake for 15 minutes. Serve immediately with whipped cream or vanilla ice cream if so desired, and sprinkle cocoa or confectioner's sugar to decorate.

Note: This recipe is for 6 standard size ramekins but can vary depending on the size.

203

Hot chocolate

Makes 4 servings

2 cups whole milk
$1^{1/2}$ cups water
$4^{1/2}$ chocolate squares
2 tablespoons sweet cocoa

Heat milk and water; add chocolate in small pieces, and stir until completely dissolved. Boil for a few minutes stirring constantly. Add cocoa and blend for 1 minute. Serve immediately and very hot.
Nothing better than sugar cookies with hot chocolate.

Sugar cookies

$1^{1/4}$ cups all-purpose flour
2 tablespoons cornstarch
1 teaspoon baking powder
1 pinch salt
1 cup sugar
7 ounces/200 g unsalted butter
1 egg yolk
$1^{1/2}$ tablespoon whipping cream

Preheat oven at 350° F/180° C.
Cover baking pan with waxed paper. Mix flour, cornstarch, baking powder, and salt.
In a separate bowl whisk sugar and butter until soft and creamy; add egg yolk and cream. Fold in dry ingredients until dough is formed. With rolling pin, extend on flat lightly floured surface until obtaining a thin sheet (1/4 inch/1/2 cm).
Cut with cookie cutters of your choice and bake for 10 to 12 minutes or until brown.

eight teatime cravings

Scones
Makes 8 or 9

2 cups all-purpose flour
3/4 teaspoon cream of tartar
1/2 teaspoon baking powder
1/2 teaspoon salt
2 teaspoons sugar (optional)
4 tablespoons butter, very cold and cut in cubes
3/4 cup whole milk

Adjust oven rack in the middle and preheat oven to
450° F/230° C.
Sift dry ingredients and put them in food processor with blade
attached. Add butter and blend until mixture resembles coarse
crumbs. Pour milk through feed tube into flour mixture until dough
is blended.
Turn dough onto well-floured surface and pat dough to a thickness
of 3/4 inch/1.5 cm
Grease and flour a 3-inch/7 cm cookie cutter and cut dough
into circles. Place on greased and floured cookie sheet
2 inches/5 cm apart.
Bake scones 12 to 14 minutes or until golden. Serve just
baked from the oven with butter, whipped cream, and/or
marmalade or jam.

208

Cheese cake with tea

Cheese cake with tea

Makes 12 to 14 servings

$2^{1/2}$ ounces/70 g melted unsalted butter
1 cup crumbs of *petit beurre* type cookies
2 pounds/1000 g cream cheese
$1^{1/2}$ cups sugar
4 large eggs
1/3 cup heavy whipping cream
1 tablespoon Earl Grey tea or tea of your taste
1/4 cup sour cream
1 cup dehydrated cranberries
Tea leaves to sprinkle (optional)
Butter to grease baking pan

212

Preheat oven to 325° F/160° C.
Cover the base of a springform pan with aluminum foil, set up pan, and grease with melted butter. Mix cookie crumbs with butter and press mixture onto bottom of pan. Place in a large roasting pan and set aside.
Beat cream cheese just until smooth; gradually beat in sugar, and continue beating until completely dissolved. Without stopping to beat, add eggs one by one.
Heat some cream with tea for 2 minutes; remove from heat and let stand at room temperature. Add the rest of the cream, the sour cream, and fold in to the cheese mixture.
Pour the mixture in the baking pan previously prepared; add cranberries on top and sprinkle some tea leaves, if so desired. Add hot water to the roasting pan until it reaches halfway up side of pan. Bake for 1 hour and 15 minutes or until edges come loose. Center may jiggle slightly. Turn oven off; let cheesecake remain in oven with door slightly open for 1 more hour. Remove from oven and cool on wire rack. Refrigerate 4 hours or until well chilled. It can be stored in the refrigerator for up to 4 days.

Note: The cranberries or the tea may be changed for other decorative ingredients of your choice.

Coconut puddings with lime and ginger

Makes 6 servings

1 egg
3 egg whites
1/8 cup water
1/2 cup sweet coconut cream
1 teaspoon vanilla extract
1 cup all-purpose flour
1/2 cup sugar
1/2 tablespoon baking powder
1 pinch salt
4 ounces/125 g unsalted butter
1 cup grated dehydrated coconut

Lime and ginger sauce

1 cup water
1/2 cup sugar
1 tablespoon lime juice
1½ teaspoon grated lime rind
1/2 teaspoon fresh ginger, grated
3/4 cup dehydrated coconut, grated and lightly toasted

Grease and flour 6 ramekins or round cups of 1/2 cup capacity. Mix egg with egg whites, water, coconut cream and vanilla extract. In separate bowl, mix flour, sugar, baking powder, and salt. Add butter in small cubes and blend with fingertips until mixture resembles coarse crumbs.

With an electric mixer, beat mixture adding liquid ingredients until obtaining a smooth and creamy mixture. Fold in coconut, and pour into ramekins. Place them in a oven safe baking pan with paper towels at the bottom, and fill with boiling water to come halfway up the sides of ramekins. Cover each with a circle of waxed paper lightly greased. Bake for 30 minutes or until knife inserted in center of pudding comes out clean.

Meanwhile make the sauceby boiling water with sugar, stirring occasionally until sugar dissolves. Add lime juice, rind, and ginger, and remove from heat.

Once cooked, remove puddings from heat and let stand for 15 minutes. Unmold and spoon some sauce over each pudding. Sprinkle lightly toasted coconut and serve hot or at room temperature.

213

Coconut puddings with lime and ginger

Blinis
Makes 8 to 10

1 $^{1/2}$ teaspoon active yeast
2 $^{1/2}$ cups lukewarm whole milk
1 teaspoon unsalted butter
1 teaspoon sugar
11 ounces/350 g all-purpose flour
3 egg yolks
1 teaspoon salt
2 tablespoons whipping cream
3 egg whites

Dissolve yeast in 1/2 cup lukewarm milk mixed with melted
butter and sugar. Let stand for a few minutes and stir until
completely dissolved.
Put flour in a large bowl; make a hole in the center and add
yeast mixture. Then add the rest of the milk in a steady stream
whisking by hand, and slowly fold in flour. Let stand for at least
15 minutes and fold in egg yolks, salt, and whipping cream.
Last, beat egg whites to soft peaks; add to mixture gently with a
plastic spatula.
Preheat a small skillet or frying pan and pour in batter as for
pancakes. Cook for 2 minutes or until brown on the base and the
surface is full of bubbles; turn over and cook 1 minute more.
Repeat this process until all the batter is used.
Serve with the side order of your taste such as sour cream with
salt and pepper, smoked salmon, caviar, etc.

Sundried tomato sandwiches / Dates and prosciutto sandwiches / Herbs and shrimp canapés

Sundried tomato sandwiches
Makes 12

1/2 cup sundried tomatoes
3/4 cup homemade mayonnaise
Salt and pepper
11 ounces/350 g bacon
1 whole bread loaf, or 6 white bread or rye slices, without edges and cut in half
1 cup lettuce, cut in small pieces

Homemade mayonnaise
1 egg yolk
1 teaspoon mustard
1 teaspoon white vinegar
1 teaspoon lime juice
3/4 cup vegetable oil
Salt and pepper to taste

220

Check the sundried tomatoes and if they are not soft, soak them briefly in hot water.

In the meantime, make the mayonnaise:

Whisk the egg yolk with mustard, vinegar and lime juice. Without stopping to beat, add oil in a steady stream. Continue beating so that the mixture thickens. Season with salt and pepper to taste.

If the tomatoes were soaked, dry them on paper towels. Place in blender with mayonnaise and blend until smooth. Season with salt and pepper.

In a hot pan fry bacon in its own fat until crisp. Drain on paper towel and break in small pieces.

With a sharp knife (an electric knife is best for this purpose), cut the top off a bread loaf. Carefully cut down inside the crust to remove the soft bread in one piece. Save the remaining bread box and the lid.

Slice the soft bread into sandwich size pieces. Spread half the slices with the tomato mixture, sprinkle with bacon, cover with lettuce and a second slice of bread. Arrange sandwiches in the bread box for serving.

For a simpler version, use sliced white or rye bread, remove crusts and make the sandwiches as above.

Dates and prosciutto sandwiches
Makes 12

1/3 cup port
3/4 cup dates, chopped
4 ounces/125 g butter, at room temperature
12 slices of bread loaf, cut in halves
12 slices prosciutto

Place port in small saucepan, and boil for 5 minutes or until it reduces by half. Remove and let stand.
Meanwhile chop dates with a knife or in food processor and mix with butter until evenly combined. Add port and chill to stiffen. Spread half the slices of bread with the butter mixture; add 1 slice prosciutto and cover with the remaining bread slices.

Herbs and shrimp canapés
Makes 12

12 shrimp, medium size
3 tablespoons extra virgin olive oil
1/4 cup chives, chopped
1/4 cup fresh basil, chopped
Salt and pepper
12 slices of bread loaf, cut in halves
2 ounces/60 g unsalted butter
1 small cucumber, thinly sliced
12 lemon wedges, peeled

Peel, clean, and open shrimp through the middle lengthwise. In a frying pan, heat oil, and sauté shrimp for a couple of minutes until they are pink. Add chives and basil. Season with salt and pepper. Spread slices of bread with butter, and place slices of cucumber on top. Then distribute shrimp and lemon wedges.

221

Mint iced tea
Makes 4 to 6 cups

5 mango tea bags or tea of your taste
4 cups bottled water, without gas
1/4 cup mint or peppermint leaves
3 tablespoons brown sugar, cane sugar or honey
4 cups ice cubes

In a saucepan, heat tea bags with water and mint leaves (slightly mashed with a wooden spoon), until it is about to boil. Remove from heat and let stand for 3 minutes. Strain, add sugar, and mix until completely dissolved. Add ice cubes and stir until they melt. Serve in glasses filled with ice and fresh peppermint.
As water from the faucet tends to cloud tea, it is preferable to use bottled water.

GLOSSARY OF SELECTED TERMS

Al dente: Italian expression that refers to the adequate point of cooking for pasta or for vegetables which indicates that food is crunchy. It literally means "to the bite".

Arugula: of very special flavor, this green vegetable is very adequate for combining with fruit and other ingredients in salads and ingenious preparations.

Baby spinach: small, tender, and of delicate flavor.

Bain Marie: special cooking system in a double pan. The larger one is placed with water over heat and the smaller one submerged inside with what is being prepared. This system allows cooking food with constant heat.

Balsamic vinegar: produced from the natural fermentation of trebbino grapes that grown in the hills of the region of Modena. The original production of this vinegar is done in the consecutive cellars of different wood that communicate its particular aroma and flavor. It is a traditional vinegar that takes 12 years to mature and the extra-mature takes 25 years. In the market, you can find industrial varieties that are more economical.

Blue cheese: appreciated variety of strong cheese, made with cow's milk, famous for its taste and aroma as well as for its texture and exotic color.

Brie cheese: soft, white cheese, originated in Brie, France.

Calvados: apple liquor, originated in Calvados, France.

Chilli oil: known also as red oil, it is a vegetable oil of an infusion done with dry red chilli. It is used as a spice in the kitchen and at the table.

Chilli: name given to a great variety of peppers, sweet or hot.

Chutney: typical from India, chutney is a mixture, generally hot, of spices, fruit, and herbs. Very popular in the world today, the different types of chutney are excellent and surprising complements.

Corn syrup: sweet and thick syrup made with cornstarch.

Cranberry: small, red, sour, creamed-colored berry, produced by one of the species of macrocarpon Vaccinium, generally used in the preparation of sweet sauces and desserts.

Crème de cassis: sweet liquor, of French origin, made with red currant. This ingredient is used often in desserts and cocktails.

Curry: name given to the aromatic and generally spicy mixture of several spices, among those cumin, cilantro, pepper, turmeric, much used for cooking in India, Thailand and Indonesia.

Dashi: basic ingredient in Japanese cooking. Dashi is the basis for broth, made with dry algae (kombu) and grated bonito fish. It is found in concentrated, instant preparation with the generic name of dashi-no-moto, ready to be dissolved in water.

Dijon mustard: valued variety of the spice, made with mustard paste and wine, which has the name of the French city where it originated.

Farfalle: variety of pasta in bow-tie form.

Fudge: soft type candy made with butter, sugar, milk and flavoring.

Ginger: aromatic and flavoring root, fundamental in the preparation of many salads and candies of the far East. It is found fresh in the market.

Gyozas: small dumplings of Japanese origin, filled with meat and vegetables that are fried or steamed. Dough to make them is found ready-made.

Hoisin sauce: its name means fresh navy. As popular in China as ketchup is in the West, it is prepared with fermented soy paste, sugar, vinegar, garlic, chilli and sesame.

Julienne: special cut of food in thin sticks.

Juniper berries: dry fruit from European tree called

juniper. It is one of the basic essentials of certain gins.

Licorice: dark extract from the plant of sweet roots that has the same name used in the preparation of candies and medications.

Marcarpone: concentrated type of cream cheese, native of the region of Lombardy, in Italy.

Mirin: sweet wine made of rice, produced in Japan only for cooking, except in the celebration of New Year when it is given a ceremonial use.

Nachos: flakes of corn tortilla, very much used in Mexican culinary preparations.

Phyllo: Dough found in sheets. It is used in Middle East pastry, of great elasticity that allows itself to be reduced to the thickness of paper.

Pine nuts: dry fruit from pine kernel pine tree, of high nutritional value, they are very popular in the diet of the Middle East.

Pita: named Arabic bread, it is a round, elastic, and thin bread, typical of the Middle East, where its consumption is as popular as bread in the West and is used to go with or fold in the preparation of meat, vegetables, and leguminous plants.

Port: sweet, dark wine of Portuguese origin.

Portobello: variety of mushrooms of fairly large size, strong texture, and excellent flavor, very much used both in Italian and French cooking.

Prosciutto: Italian ham cured by drying, cut in very thin slices.

Ricotta: literally rice in Italian, it is the name given to the preparations of rice originated or inspired in the kitchen in this part of the world. They are famous for its flavors and the varied incorporation of ingredients to rice.

Rose water: water made with rose essence. It is a flavoring very popular in the Middle East.

Sage: spice of intense aroma and flavor, very much used as a spice in sauce and fillings.

Sesame oil: dark and thick oil made with sesame seeds.

Setas: type of mushroom, of large size, very much used in culinary for its excellent taste.

Shiitake: very old mushroom of Japanese origin, very popular for its excellent flavor and its medicinal proprieties. It is the second most cultivated in the world.

Sour cream: very thick whipping cream of acid taste.

Soy sauce: the most common of all the sauces in the kitchen and table in Japan, China and the rest of the East. It has an innumerous variety and types.

Sumak: red, dark spice in powder, made from the BAYA of the bush that carries its name, much appreciated in the Middle East for its citric taste. It is used in the preparation of meat, bread, and salads.

Szechwan pepper: originated from the Chinese province of Szechwan, this spice, although its name is not related to current pepper, has a fragrance and a special taste that is totally different to that of common pepper and chilli.

Tempura: name given to the frying of vegetables, fish or seafood coated in a mixture of sifted all-purpose flour with egg and water.

Teriyaki: one of the most popular and versatile sauces of Japanese cooking, it is a mixture of equal amount of mirin and soy sauce. It is used to marinate, glaze or go with.

Turmeric: ground root from a tropical plant of intense, yellow color and wood flavor, turmeric or cúrcuma is one of the ingredients of many types of curry.

Vermicelli: very thin pasta known also as cellophane noodles, made with mung bean flour. When submerged in hot water, they become transparent.

Vongole: Italian name for clam.

Zucchini: Italian name for green summer squash.

227

INDEX OF RECIPES

INDEX OF SELECTED INGREDIENTS